daodejing 道德经

daodejing 道德经

an interpretation by:
David Breeden
Wally Swist
Steven Schroeder

with images by:
Mary Ann O'Donnell
Steven Schroeder

ISBN: 978-0-9915321-7-9
Library of Congress Control Number: 2015930153
Printed in the United States of America

Book design: forgetgutenberg.com
Cover design and cover painting: stevenschroeder.org
Interior photos: Mary Ann O'Donnell
Interior paintings: Steven Schroeder

Lamar University Press
Beaumont, Texas

coast : lines

coast : lines
danger, do not go to sea

coast : lines
old border station

coast : lines
drying shrimp

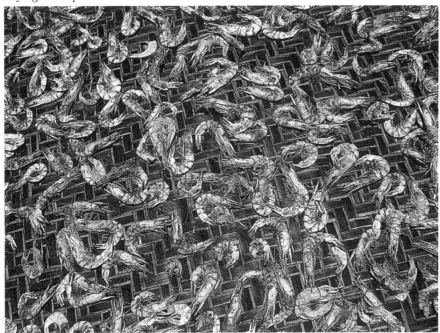

coast : lines
facing sea road

coast : lines
worker

coast : lines
sea world

coast : lines
shekou sea world

UNDISPUTED POSSESSION
OF THE WORLD

家在·情在

Home is where the heart is

招商地產

coast : lines
undisputed possession

by way of introduction...

IN THE United States, three poets came together to offer three translations of the Dao De Jing. Why would they do so? After all, there is already a website, *Dao is Open*, that not only places over twenty English-language translations of the *Dao De Jing* in conversation, but also sells a product called *Your Dao De Jing*, which facilitates personalized translations of the text's 81 chapters. The materials comprising *Your Dao De Jing* include a version in both traditional and simplified characters, the Wade-Giles and pinyin romanizations for each character, and brief English definitions for each character. Two assumptions—one explicit, one implicit—inform the compilation of translation resources in *Your Dao De Jing*. First, the author assumes that translation entails moving from a Chinese character to an English word. Second, the author relies on a long history of previous English language translations to contextualize those character/words. It is a dazzling moment of imploding assumptions—*Your Dao De Jing* is simultaneously a jigsaw puzzle comprised of decontextualized Chinese characters and an always already present English text. And yet. The 道德经 effortlessly escapes a final form because English grammar and 21st century technologies cannot provide safe passage between Chinese fragments, the canonical specter of Ezra Pound withstanding. In fact, it is an open question if Modern Chinese grammar would offer a clear map for navigating the distance between Lao Zi then and now, let alone that between "the Old One" here and there.

Understanding begins in and returns to water.

Lao Zi assumed that objects were not only material, but also expressed a virtue or moral being that are proper to themselves and the most virtuous of all objects was water—the highest good is water, he claimed. Water doesn't oppose anything. It adapts to whatever it encounters, flowing over riverbeds or forming waves when wind blows across the ocean surface. It freezes, condenses, and can become steam. The question for those of us in the Anglophone West (and especially for our translators) is: what to make of the expression, "the highest good is water"? Are we to be like water (making metaphoric sense of the Chinese)? Or might we take the expression "the highest good is water" literally and posit a virtue or virtues proper to every material form (extrapolating instructions for translation from the nature of water)?

One of the key paradoxes in the *Dao De Jing* describes water: that which is soft overcomes that which is strong. When we think of "soft" and "hard" with respect to water, we realize that Lao Zi reminds us that the formless (because water takes the shape of whatever it encounters) eventually overcomes that which has a fixed form, such as a rock. In fact, we hear echoes of this virtuous logic throughout the *Dao De Jing*: "take the fraudulent as being true" and "take the passive as being active." In what sense is the fraudulent true? Perhaps the fraudulent is never truer than when we are "keeping up appearances." The appearance may not be an accurate representation of a situation, but it does accurately reflect that we think the situation should be. Similarly, we might ask: when does passivity become active virtue? As the civil rights movement taught us, non-cooperation may more effectively transform society than armed resistance, especially when our goal is not to destroy our neighbors, but rather to restructure our relationship with them. But all this thinking is latent in the fluidity of metaphor which directs the mind through association rather than predication. Objective form, Lao Zi reminds us, is everywhere inconsistent and so that which most readily changes—water—is itself the realization of the highest virtue.

Consider what happens when we understand the *Dao De Jing* to actualize a "true being" or "natural morality" proper to texts. Classical Chinese scholarship, for example, holds translation to three standards—信 (xìn), 达 (dá), and 雅 (yǎ). Each of these terms both refers to an aspect of language and a feature of social relationships. Xìn, for example, comprises characters meaning "person" and "tongue or speech" and is the last of the five constant Confucian virtues (rújiào wǔcháng), which are traditionally listed as: benevolence, righteousness, ritual, wisdom, and trust. It refers to the idea that an interlocutor can believe that our words point to truth because they are an extension of our moral being, which is faithful to the original meaning of a text. In turn, the primary meaning of dá is arrival or a conduit. Dá also appears in verbs meaning to express, to manifest, and to understand, as well as in nominal phrases referring to high-ranking people, who have 'arrived', so to speak. With respect to translation dá is the vehicle that connects a text (the *Dao De Jing*, for example) to an unintended audience (21ˢᵗ century North Americans). This social fact bears repeating. Once upon a time, the *Dao De Jing* circulated among readers (Chinese literati) who could be expected not only to read the text without translation, but also to understand it within and against a particular understanding of how language itself was a manifestation of nature (more below). For the moment, it is important simply to note that dá is not a simple technique, but like xìn forces readers to acknowledge that translation entails entering a social relationship between an implied author and a new audience—indeed, the conduit simultaneously mediates and constitutes this audience. Finally, of the three classical standards of translation, yǎ most explicitly draws our attention to the social temporality of a literary vehicle, referring to both standard and elegance. On the one hand, yǎ describes correct and proper forms. On the other hand, yǎ designates stylish and sophisticated forms. Significantly, the tension between the correct and the elegant highlights how translation is socially produced because yǎ does more than alert the reader to the fact that for any word (let alone text) there is more than one possible translation. Instead, yǎ makes salient the difference between accuracy and elegance as values held by different groups of translators and their intended readers. Moreover, our capacity as translators to create believable translations often hinges on how we (and our readers) rank accuracy and beauty as values of linguistic practice.

The Daoist understanding of the material world as virtuous expression figures the proliferation of Dao De Jing translations as attempts to re/establish correct human relationships. This understanding emphasizes the inherent morality of language in its material form. In fact, the canonical version of the Dao De Jing must be understood against the larger cultural framing of language as a material expression of virtuous relationships. The ancient Chinese state criminalized the use of the emperor's given name and those of his ancestors. This practice was called "naming taboo (名讳)" and entailed the rewriting of texts to expunge tabooed characters on the ascension of a new Emperor. Sometimes, characters were altered or substitutions made to bring a text into accordance with the law. Other times, a benevolent Emperor whose birth name included a common character would change his name to a less commonly used character. As late as 1777, Wang Xihou compiled a dictionary in which he wrote the Qianlong Emperor's name. This violation resulted in his and his family's executions as well as the confiscation of their property.

For the purposes of this introduction, it is interesting to consider two implications of the naming taboo on the actual text of the Dao De Jing as well as its possible translations. First, the earliest version of the Dao De Jing, for example, began with the line "道可道

非恒道". However, during the reign of the Han Wen Di Emperor (ruled 179-157 BC), the fifth character of the line "permanent or eternal (恒 héng)" was changed to "often or constant (常 cháng)" because the birth name of the Han Wen Di Emperor (202-157 BC) was "恒". The opening line was rewritten as the now canonical "道可道非常道". Importantly, the distance between 恒 and 常 has physical form, or as it is called in Chinese a "body (体)" and this "body" is an expression of virtuous relationships. The character for "eternal" comprises pictographs of a heart (心) that crosses a river on a small boat, presumably with ferryman (亘). In contrast, the character for "usual" combines a piece of cloth (巾) beneath a phonetic marker for the sound "shàng" (尚). In ancient Chinese a 常 referred to a ruler's banner. Clearly, 恒 and 常 referred to substantively different socialities. 恒 evoked an individual's existential being, while 常 referred to an institution's political being. The question that confronts a translator is: in what moral imaginary are existential and political terms for "a long time" synonymous? And just how seriously should a translator take a character substitution that occurred over two thousand years ago? Second, the fifth character of the second line of the text, "名可名非常名" was not only changed from "eternal" to "often or usual", but also literally true—the name that could be named was in fact not the eternal or usual name of exalted personages. In other words, the current text of the *Dao De Jing* was itself liquid, flowing around and over linguistic taboos in order to point to something that was both eternal and ordinary, ineffable and yet formed in ~~language~~ social relationships.

The importance of embodied virtue becomes apparent when we turn our gaze from individual characters to the first sentence of the text (as inherited by Chinese readers): "道可道非常道". English speakers may have encountered this sentence as, "The Way that can be spoken of is not the true Way." We have been taught to be in the world but not of it, and our meta-language assumes that existential questions belong to a sphere outside the state. For a native English speaker, then, especially one raised in the United States, where Church and State have (in theory) been separated, the sentence "the Way that can be spoken of is not the true Way" points to a mode of being beyond or external to society. Moreover, we acknowledge that there are moments when this "higher morality" supersedes those of the state. We just don't agree on when those moments have occurred.

In contrast, Chinese readers inherited the sentence "the Way that can be spoken of is not the true Way" through a meta-language that assumed that correct language actualized proper social relationships; as water and characters have a body, so too does society. Consequently, classical Chinese meta-language assumed moral immanence (rather than its externalization). Achieving a moral life did not entail realizing an otherworldly truth, but understanding one's role with respect to another. In this sense, "the Way that can be spoken of is not the true way" offers instruction in human relationships, begging the question: why not? The answer becomes clear when we consider that classical Chinese morality demanded appropriate action in a given social situation—how fathers treated sons, or wives obeyed their husbands, for example. If this immanent morality sounds suspiciously Confucian it is because Lao Zi and Confucius lived and developed their philosophies in and against the same cultural values. What appears as the difference between the two ancients is what might be understood in colloquial English as a debate over whether there's been too much talk and not enough walk. Lao Zi pointedly pointed out that Confucians gave lip service to proper social relationships, when true virtue was in fact expressed through action. Did you bow when you were supposed to? Did you offer tea to your guest?

The importance of embodied action as the true expression of the Dao is even clearer when we remember that in Bronze character versions of the Dao De Jing, the character 道 was often used in place of the homophone 导 (dǎo). In traditional Chinese, this character is written as 導 placing the character for right hand beneath the character for path or way. So where 道 refers to a path, the character 導 makes explicit that our relationship to that path is a wordless social relationship—one either points out the correct direction, or on taking direction one steps forward. The poignancy of Lao Zi's wordless ethics becomes salient in the next sentence, "the Name that can be spoken (or named) is not the true Name." After all, commoners could not use the Emperor's name—their virtue is expressed by knowing when to keep silent.

In obvious contrast to the Chinese folk understanding of language as an expression of immanent social body (organized through proper modes of relating), Richard Rorty (1979) has argued that Anglophones have traditionally understood language as a "mirror of nature". Two assumptions inform this assumption. First, we assume that language represents objects in the material world as mental objects. Second, we have also assumed that these mental representations correspond to objects in the material world. In this sense, language (mental images) "mirrors" nature (objects). The philosophical roots of this assumption can be traced to Platonic forms, where an eternal (or constant) form predicated the meaning of actual (or inconstant) objects. If we return to the first line of the *Dao De Jing,* we can see how this understanding structures an Anglophone translation project such as the *Your Dao De Jing.* First, the Chinese text is reduced to "characters" which can be represented as "words" that in turn refer back to some kind of disembodied (yet eternal) Chinese form. For example, if we assume that 道 refers to the word "path" or "way", we imagine an eternal form—the way—that has concrete manifestations in the world. This can be an actual "path" or "the way (or manner)" in which we cross the path. But here's the rub: by equating characters to words (a way of translation) we lose the material virtue—the water—that flows throughout the 道德经 as a Chinese text. The question facing our three translators and you the reader has been posed by Gregory Bateson: does this difference make a difference, and what are we to make of it?

Mary Ann O'Donnell and Yang Qian
Shenzhen, China
July 2014

I AM a Daodejing junky. I have read every translation that I have managed to get my hands on. I buy new ones when they are published.

The following is my reading of the *Daodejing*. I have read the *Daodejing* as a spiritual practice every day for many years. For the past several years, I have done this reading with a word-processing file open, working on my own version. When I got the chance to read two more translations—this time in the matrix of creativity produced by watching two poets (also *Daodejing* junkies!) working on the *Daodejing* chapter by chapter with me—I was overjoyed.

In one way, the *Daodejing* is infuriating: the text merely turns the obvious on its head, claiming that the culturally conditioned response is wrong—is out of balance with the way of the universe. Also, the sayings often fall into the Golden Age Fallacy: that things were done correctly in the past, and if we'd just return to the Good Ol' Days, all would be well.

Despite these faults, the *Daodejing* has great power. I suspect that this power (falling into my own Golden Age Fallacy, perhaps) stems from the fact that the text is an elegant summary of ancient, shamanistic, revelation...a worldwide phenomenon.

So much of earth-based spirituality has been edited out of Western philosophy and religion that the words of the Dao sound like divine revelation. Yet, at base, the wisdom of the *Daodejing* lies in its simple evocation of the ways of nature, of the creativity of the cosmos. Water runs downhill! Westerners are fascinated to hear something that sounds so simple, yet is so easily forgotten.

The most profound lesson of the *Daodejing*, however, is what it does not say. It does not claim that the universe has meaning or purpose. We learn how to find our own meaning and purpose by observing the universe, but that is merely human meaning and purpose. The Way goes on, heedless of the human quest for meaning.

We forget these simple and profound revelations to our peril.

David Breeden
Minneapolis, Minnesota
March 2014

MY PROCESS

MY PROCESS was initially reading the translation that Steve would post, which I would then copy into my hardcover journal whose sole purpose was a workbook for *Daodejing*. My approach was to place my self in the forefront of Steve's translation with an amount of veneration, then, and this was always crucial, to find, and more appropriately discover, where the lyric core of the poem arose from. When I found that, then my own rendering flowed. However, it may have been one or two of the middle lines, perhaps an image at the end, and most usually, especially toward the conclusion of *Daodejing*, with the beginning lines, that I was able to locate the *source* of the flow of each particular verse.

My attempt was not only to render 'our old teacher,' Laozi, but to play off of Steve's translation—much like how John Coltrane released the sweet torrent of sound from his saxophone in harmonizing with Johnny Hartman's voice, and Johnny Hartman's debonair baritone rising to meet that effusion of Coltrane's grace notes—but also my purpose was to limn Steve's meaning; to shadow a phrase, here and there; and to offer both clarity and a mirror to the perpetuity of the sage's import and wisdom.

Steve's invitation for me to participate in this interactive rendering of Dao, is a watershed event for me—one in which I have prepared for all of my writing life. I am grateful for the opportunity to work with both Steve Schroeder and David Breeden, who both provided the appropriate alchemy for my own lyrical contributions to the project. I first came across the Gia-Fu Feng and Jane English translation of Laozi when I was twenty, over forty years ago in New Haven, when I was also reading every Eastern classic I could assimilate, as well as practicing Zazen with a small group of people in the basement of Yale Divinity School Chapel. Although I augmented my reading of Steve's translations with the Feng and English version, and often enough chose to strike a balance between the two to actually and effectively fashion a new rendering, I have also treasured Ursula K. LeGuin's translation, as well as Stephen Mitchell's, who, on occasion, as I recall, was one of the other participants in sitting meditation in the basement at the Divinity School Chapel, when he was grad student at Yale.

So, my being invited to render Laozi has been completing an enormous circle for me, as Joseph Campbell, whose voluminous works of comparative religion and mythology I have studied, might point out as being the hero's journey. In that time it is not only

Campbell who I found both inspiration and guidance from, much after my discovery of Laozi, but also the psycho-spirituality of the modern mystic Carolyn Myss, and the high octane spirituality of The Guide Lectures, channeled by Eva Pierrakos, among many others, whose writing regarding higher consciousness have affected me, such as Pema Chodron, Katherine MacCoun, and Eckhart Tolle—all of whose insights, at least partially, I have integrated, and that have lent themselves to becoming some of the very philosophical underpinnings of my renderings of Daodejing.

It is with gratitude, and an active humility, that I thank everyone here that I have mentioned by name, including, of course, 'our old teacher,' and offer a deep appreciation for the verses themselves, as well as for Yinxi, the sentry at the western gate, who, aprocryphally or not, stopped Laozi, and asked him to record his wisdom before moving on, into the frontier, beyond, which as a result was Daodejing—for it is as if I have come to meet them both, stepping out of the western frontier of the future, to greet them in the eternal now of the present, in which we all have come together, with our hands placed firmly palm to palm, bowing to one another, in unison, not to affect benefit for ourselves, but for the positive intent and good will of every reader.

Wally Swist
South Amherst, Massachusetts
March 2014

I FIRST encountered Laozi forty years ago in the beautiful translation by Gia-Fu Feng and Jane English. I was an undergraduate at Valparaiso University at the time, but I had the advantage of reading him out of class as a happy discovery – one of those chance encounters with a stranger that turns into a lifelong friendship. The Chinese calligraphy and photos that accompanied the translation made it a visually memorable experience, and the Colorado mountains placed the text in familiar territory – not quite home, but close.

The traditional story of how this text came to be didn't much register at the time; but it has come to be more important to me as I have crossed more borders. As the story goes, the character who came to be known simply as "old teacher" had been an aparatchik in the imperial court but headed west when he grew sick of politics. When he arrived at the western frontier, a guard recognized him and demanded that he write down his teaching before he could pass. I've had enough border encounters to have a clear vision of an eighteen year old kid with a Kalashnikov demanding something in a place where there are not many common words – so it's not hard for me to imagine the old teacher sampling and remixing freely if that's what it would take to get him over.

That this wonderfully mystical text is so deeply rooted in a place of few words and intent on finding what it takes to be on one's way has shaped my reading of mysticism since. It is about this, that, and the other, making our way, and it is a masterpiece of making do. That is exactly what I expect of a philosophy of language in a world such as ours where friends and strangers standing in the way often demand our full attention.

Still, we carry on.

This begins, I think, as a sort of parallel play...

I began by posting a rough translation of each verse as I read it, making my way with very limited Chinese, staying as close to what I thought the old master said as I thought I could in English.

And moves toward play in conversation...

After reading what Wally and David posted, I tried again, this time straying a bit further into poetry. And then I turned to a wider circle—conversations with Sou Vai Keng and Huichun Liang, discussion with students in the Asian Classics program at the University of Chicago Graham School, translations by Gia-Fu Feng and Jane English, Red Pine, Chad Hansen, and others—and tried again.

That third pass, often repeated again and again—a reading in English that takes the form of poetry in conversation with a circle of friends with what little we know of the old master in mind—is my contribution to the present work.

But what matters in all of this is the silence between lines, the kind of silence that is possible between friends. Just between you and me, between is where I would direct your attention in Laozi and in what follows.

Steven Schroeder
Chicago, Illinois
March 2014

I:
DAO

I

Talking the talk is not walking
the walk. Naming a name means another
name. Name nothing, and the world begins.
Naming is the mother of ten thousand things.

Desire nothing, see wonder.
Desire more, see nothing
but what you happen

to see. One source, two names.
Say wonder, say wonder, say
wonder again. Open a door
on wonder upon wonder.

A way that
can be walked
is off the way
of the universe.

A name that
can be named
blots the
lasting name.

Without name, the way
is origin of all that is;
named, a way creates
all we see.

Reaching, we find edges.

Without reaching,
we find essence.

All has the same source;
only the names
and the naming disagree.

Mystery has two ways—
naming and not naming.

Mystery itself is
the gate to knowing.

Walking the way is not the true walk
of the way.
When we speak the name of the way,
it is not the real name.

When everything began, it grew out of
the name;
and the name of the word is
the mother of the ten thousand things.

When we desire nothing, we see what is;
when we want more, we become blind.
What transpires, transpires, as a spring—
and the fountain runs, from the source.

However, there are two names for
what is but one; the one that is whole—
when these are found together,
we enter a realm of mystery.

This mystery opens
when we no longer see it as mystery—
again, on its threshold,
the door to self is no door at all.

Everyone knows beauty as beauty
because there is something they despise.

The good is known as good
because there is no good.

Having and not having
give birth to each other.

Hard and easy
change into each other.

Long and short
shape each other.

High and low
rest on each other.

Sound and voice
blend.

Front and back
follow each other.

The work of the sage is to do nothing,
to go about teaching not talking.

Ten thousand things come and go.
Give birth and there is nothing

to rely on. Dwell on nothing
and it will not pass away.

2

Those who boast that they know beauty
spurn the beautiful, and make it repulsive.
Those who claim to know the good,
as good, breed arrogance. What is emerges
from what is not; and although both are

opposites, each depends on the other.
What is difficult becomes easy, and what
is simple never refrains from being hard.
Length is measured as much by how long
it is as by how often it comes up short.

What is elevated recedes; whoever is
knocked down has reason enough to stand
up again. The cellist releases the mystic
voice of the cello through long practice.
When she sleeps with her front to my back,

I awaken to the warmth of her breasts
pressing against me. The sage's advice
is to not do anything, and echoes this
by teaching without pedantry.
The ten thousand things are both nascent

and passing—all at once. We need to let go,
if we want to become one with what *is*.
Whatever it is that we seek, we must learn
to let go of any notion of letting go,
for us to be resilient enough to receive it.

When we see beauty,
we know of ugliness.

When we recognize
the excellent, we know
there is shoddy.

Seen and unseen flow
from each other.

The difficult and the easy
go 'round and around.

Long and short;
high and low;

before and after;
noise and music—

each exists because
of the other.

This is why those free
of themselves act
without expectations,
teach without words.

In every action
they act according to
the will of the action.

They act without fuss,
but act in power.

Not thinking themselves worthy means
people have nothing to fight about.

Not possessing expensive things means
people have nothing to steal.

Not looking with desire means
people's hearts are not confused.

The wise rule by emptying hearts,
stuffing bellies, weakening wills,
strengthening bones.

The people neither know
nor desire, and the wise don't dare.

So that nothing will happen,
have nothing to control.

3

Not believing that you are worthy
gives no one a reason to fight about

whether or not you are unworthy.
Not possessing what is expensive

offers reason not to steal.
Not looking at what is desirous

cinctures the heart.
The wise rule by emptying the hearts

of the people and by
filling their bellies; by subjugating

their ambition and by making
their bones strong. If people find

themselves unaware, they instinctively
desire knowledge. Those who are

wise practice the art of wei wu wei—
doing nothing about doing nothing.

So, when nothing is happening,
everything is in order;

and there is *nothing* to resist—
there is no need to exercise control.

Why promote
the upper crust
when it only leads
to wrangling?

When fancy things
are not prized,
no one steals.

Desire for things
leads to disorder.

Those free of themselves
encourage peaceful minds
out for only basic needs.

When grasping stops,
the bones get strong.

Sages discourage contriving
and desire, and when some

contrive and desire,
sages put a stop to it.

By embracing harmony,
they create
good order everywhere.

Dao is empty,
used but not filled,
an abyss like the ancestor
of ten thousand things.

Bend the edge,
untangle the knot,
blend light with dust.

Clear as though present,
I do not know whose child it is.

It is as though it was
before the first emperor.

4

If dao is a vessel, it is empty;
if it is used, it can never be filled.

If dao is an abyss, its ancestor
is original emptiness.

If dao is a source, it is the spring
of ten thousand things.

Blunt what is sharp;
unravel what is snarled;

merge as dust motes
infuse a column of sunlight;

make clear what is ever-present.
If dao is a child, whose child is it?

Oh, it wanders endlessly,
even long before the forgotten

memories of the first emperor's
forefather—

always at home in the world,
preceding earliest history.

The way of the creative universe
is emptiness. It never fills up.

It is deep, the source of everything.
It blunts edges, untangles knots;

it blends light and dark and
brings all things into harmony.

The way goes on and on.
I do not know whose child

it is; it just was, before
the oldest of ancestors.

The world, heartless,
uses the ten thousand things
as straw dogs.

The sage, heartless,
uses common people
as straw dogs.

Is the space between
heaven and earth
not like a bellows?

Empty but unyielding,
every motion makes more—
but more talk makes poor,
inferior to what is
guarded inside.

5

It is said disinterest kills passion and stifles love,
and those who dwell in the world

toss the ten thousand things as they would
straw dogs into the gutter, after their purposes

are finished.
After the ceremony is over, even the sage

has been seen throwing a straw dog among
the real curs that prowl the cobbles of the street.

It is also said that the people choose to follow
the sage in treating other people as straw dogs.

Is not the dynamic between heaven and earth
much like a forge that is fanned by a bellows?

The answer is that maybe it is—
and that its shape may change

but what is formless doesn't change at all.
However, like spring mist,

the more we pursue it, the farther it moves away;
and the more we attempt to define it with words,

the more undefinable it remains.
We must learn to listen

to true guidance, to what it is inside us
that facilitates our locating

the center, especially after we have found it—
since it *moves*.

Heaven and earth
don't give a damn.

The universe treats everything
like so many straw dogs.

Just so the rulers of the earth
treat others like
so many straw dogs.

The space between
sky and earth is empty,
like a bellows, moving

and moving—always
out puffs more, more.

Take care of what
is within yourself:

the outside will
never stop moving

and moving.

Valley spirit never dies.
We call it a mysterious woman.
This mysterious woman is a door we call
the world: like a silk veil, used but not used up.

What is eternal is valley spirit.
It is known as a mysterious woman—

descendant of the great mother.
Such a woman of mystery is a door—

a door that opens to the world,
to what is primal:

a silk veil flowing on and on—
diaphanous, barely visible.

Use it, and it will never fail you.
Allow yourself to use it, wisely.

Permit it to guide you.
It can never be used up.

The valley spirit never dies;
this is the dark mystery.

The gate of the dark is
the source of the world.

Delicate, hidden power
flowing on and on.

Heaven and earth endure.
Heaven and earth last forever.
They last because they are unborn.

So the sage pulls back and is ahead.
He is outside his life, but his life lives.
Seeking nothing, he gains much.

7

What perpetuates is heaven and earth.
Why do heaven and earth endure?

What is unborn instinctively knows the way,
as with the sage, the same is true—

in drawing into solitude, as the sage's life
deepens.

The aloneness is austere, living on the fringe,
but as the sage's life opens, through practice,

the sage experiences the coalescence—
as all is one.

Only when we seek nothing do we have
everything to gain, do we attain fulfillment—

as the draft that issues
through a crack in the sage's creaking door.

Earth and sky have existed
a long time because they
do not exist for themselves.

Learning from this, those free
of themselves put themselves
last, yet find themselves first—

those free of themselves
forget themselves,
yet find all is well.

Selflessness leads to
understanding the self.

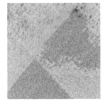

The highest good is like water.
Water is good for ten thousand things.

It does not fight. It makes its place
in the place everyone despises.
It is on the right track.

Dwell on good earth,
think deeply,
act kindly,
speak truly,
govern justly,
manage competently,

move in good time.
No fight, no blame.

8

What is the highest good?
The highest good is like water.

Water nourishes the ten thousand things.
It does not strive.

It flows—
in places most people find out of the way.

It resembles the highest good—
as does dao.

To dwell, take ease when
woodswalking the splendor of the land.

To think, penetrate the heart's lyre.
To act, respond to others from within

your own center, with love.
To speak, be kind, enunciate distinctly.

To influence, remember
a container holding the shape of water.

To succeed, when
doing business, do so with integrity.

To find your destiny,
exercise presence moment to moment.

Don't fight—
it's no lie, there's no one to blame.

Learn from water.
It benefits all as it seeks
the lowest places
without expectations.

For a house, the question
is location. For the mind,
the question is depth.

When it comes to giving,
nature is the model;

when it comes to speaking,
it is care with words.

Governing, it's about order;
in business, it's about
how to use time.

The wise do not wrangle,
nor do they judge.

Better to stop at full than to pour more.
Sharper does not mean longer lasting.
Fill a house with treasure,
and no one can protect it.

No one can protect wealth and vanity
from the blame that follows them.
Retire when your work is done.
This is heaven's way.

9

Whether pouring water or wine,
it is best to the fill glass but to stop short of the brim.
Honing the knife's

edge beyond its capacity for sharpness dulls the blade.
Accrue what is priceless,
and you will never be able to hire enough guards to

protect it.
Acquire silver, inherit gold, or become court poet—
however, you will never be able to exonerate yourself

from the concatenation
of calamities that will hound you like your own shadow.
When the work is finished,

know that it is time to put away the tools—
know that
this is not only the true way, but the way of heaven.

Fill a cup too full
and it spills.

Keep sharpening a point,
and it becomes dull.

A house filled treasure
is not safe.

When wealth and honors
plant arrogance,
the harvest is tragedy.

The way of the creative
universe lies in doing

the work, then knowing
when to stop.

Seeking the dark soul,
embracing the one,
can you keep it
together?

Can you breathe soft as a baby?
Can you cleanse your dark vision,
be without blemish?

Loving your country,
can you govern the people
without being clever?

Can you be the woman at heaven's gate?

Understanding all
four corners of the world,
can you be ignorant? Giving birth
to beings – giving birth but not possessing,
not controlling, not slaughtering.
We call this dark de.

IO

Are you able to persevere through
the dark night and to become aware that what follows any
brightness of magnitude is always requisite to darkness;
are you able to keep what is one whole;

can you become a child again—
and to see with such clarity, that it is not so far removed
from having recently been in the bardo;
are you able to clean the corroded lens of your original

vision; can the stain be rinsed away;
are you able to love every man, and
in so doing, equitably rule your country, without artifice;
are you able to become like a woman empowered,

standing beside the gates of heaven, knowing
the winds of the four directions, and to be open to them;
is it possible for you to reclaim your innocence again,
and to honor the way, by doing nothing;

can you give birth to and nourish
whom you have given life to, without possessing them;
are you able to work, but to not take credit for what is
your own inimitably fine craftsmanship;

can you influence, with confidence, but not directly
command? All of this, as impossible as it sounds, is—
the meaning of de, it is what is known as mysterious,
is active virtue as favorable darkness.

Can body and mind embrace?
With attention to the breath,
we can become gentle.

With attention to thoughts,
we clear away flaws.

Loving people and leading
must be done without pride.

The sky's gate opens and shuts
in birth and in death,
yin and yang changing,

and on. And on.

Those free of themselves
see in all directions; very
clearly they are wise.

The way of the creative universe
creates and nourishes. Yet it
does not demand or boast.

The way accomplishes everything,
yet makes no claims at all.

It rules over all
without controlling
anything.

This is the mystery
of the way.

Thirty spokes make a wheel, but
nothing makes it work.

A pot is made of clay, but
nothing makes it work.

Chisel a door in a room, and
nothing makes it work.

Profit comes from what is there, but
nothing makes it work.

II

The wheel's hub contains thirty spokes;
however, they all revolve around

the empty space at the center.
Throw a pot of clay; shape it into an urn—

what is useful is the emptiness to be filled
within.

Cut a space in a room
for a door; install jambs and screws

to hang it—
it is the emptiness created through which

you will walk, as it swings open.
We benefit from

what is inherent within.
We find what is useful from what is not.

No matter how many spokes
a wheel may have, it is the hole
at the center that makes it work.

Clay makes cups and bowls,
yet it is the hollowness that
makes them useful.

Walls make a room, yet
the empty space between
is where we live.

What is there
is useful;

what is not there
is useful too.

Five colors make the eye
blind. Five tones make the ear
deaf. Five flavors make the mouth
numb. Racing and hunting make the mind
mad. Hard to get things get in our way,
so the sage follows the gut.
not the eye, lets that go
to get this.

12

Too many colors
confuse the sight;
too many flavors
numb the mouth;

too much music
deafens; a wild
chase shakes
the mind;

precious objects
rob the will.

So, those free
of themselves
satisfy the belly,

not the eye.
Ignoring one,

the other
proves easy.

What blinds the eye?—the five colors;
and what about the ear,
how are we made deaf?—the five tones;

then what could dull
our taste, the palate, our tongue?—
nothing other than the five flavors;

so, what makes our mind
seethe with the carbides of madness—
that makes it race, always the pedal

to the floor, hurtling us through
space, in our pursuit of those thoughts
which turn on us?—isn't this what

hunts us down? Whatever
we overvalue, anything we hold
precious, leads us away from what is

intrinsic, from the original source—
but it is the sage who hears
the voice within, and listens—to what?

To let go of all that— like *the radiant,*
streaking the sky with a shower
of Perseids—choose to get to this.

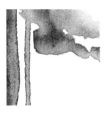

Being lifted up and being put down are alarming.
Honor and great suffering are life.

13

Why say being lifted up
and being put down are alarming?
Being lifted up leads to being put down.

To need it is alarming.
To lose it is alarming.
So we say being lifted up
and being put down are alarming.

Why speak of honor and suffering as life?
There is suffering because I am alive.
if I were not alive would I suffer?

Devote your life to the whole world
as if the whole world lived in it.
Love the whole world for the sake of life,
and the whole world may be entrusted to you.

What do we fear more than anything else?
Not so much our being raised up, in honor,

as being put down, in humiliation.
What are two truths in life?—

both high honor and deep suffering augment us,
irrevocably.

So, why be so accepting of humiliation?
Great honor leads us to the depths of suffering.

To covet great honor is abhorrent; to lose such
honor is abominable.

This is what is
known as acceptance of humiliation, with grace.

We suffer because we are alive;
If we weren't in our bodies, we wouldn't suffer.

So, why should we talk with such abandon—
honor being as flimsy as a placard—

for our suffering to reach such painful depths?
With humility,

that accrued sweetness from the hive,
give yourself up to all things in the world,

as if your entire life depended on it.
For the sake of your life,

love the world this way and everything in it.
In this way, the world, in its splendor,

may be yours to inherit,
as a bee works loose the pollen in every flower.

Fear disgrace; fear favor;
consider honor and rejection
equal in every way.

What does it mean to fear
both favor and disgrace?

It means respect for both.

What does it mean to say
"consider honor and rejection
equal in every way"?

It means living contains both.

Those who lead others
as they lead themselves

and lead themselves
with care

can be trusted to lead.

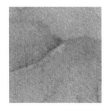

Looking not seeing.
say formless.

Listening not hearing,
say faint.

Grasping not holding,
say subtle.

These three failed
ways to know
blend into one,
no light above,
no shadow below.

Unnameable thread
returns to nothing.
This is the form of no
form, the image of no image.

Meet it, see no beginning.
Follow it, see no end.

Grasp the ancient dao
for the sake of now.

To know the ancient beginning
is the discipline of dao.

14

We look, yet do not see,
and so we say the way
is hard to see.

We listen, yet do not hear,
and so we say
it is hard to hear.

We grasp at it, yet
do not hold it,
and so name it
"too hard to hold."

Despite all these words,
All That Is is not named:

Its top is not shiny;
its bottom is not dark.

It's always in action,
yet it never moves.

It is the form of the formless;
it is a sight of the invisible.

It is the vague,
undetermined.

We meet it coming
but do not see it;

we follow it going
but do not see it.

When we manage to
get hold of the way
of the creative universe—
doing things now
as they were done
before time began—

this is called
unleashing the way.

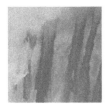

What are we looking at but not seeing—
because it is without form?
What are we listening to but not hearing—
because it is so faint it is not audible?

What is unable to be grasped if we try to hold it—
because its subtleties can't be placed in the hand?
Since these three ways of knowing have failed,
they merge into one.

From above, there is no light;
from below, there is no shadow—
what is unnamable can't be described,
even though it is joined by the common thread

of nothingness.
It is form without form;
it is an image that is imageless—
indecipherable and inscrutable fall short of what

is on the other side of the imagination.
If we could meet it, it would have no beginning.
If could follow it, it would have no end.
If we were able to comprehend

how ancient dao is—
we would need to master being present, now.
However, in coming to know its ancient beginning
is the essential discipline of dao.

Ancient masters were subtle,
mysterious, open, unfathomably
deep because they were
unfathomable.

We can only describe their appearance:

Careful as if crossing a bridge in winter,
alert as one aware of danger,
courteous as though
they were guests
giving way like ice melting,
simple as a block of wood,
open as a valley,
murky as a mud puddle.

Who can wait for the mud to settle?
Who can wait while it slowly clears?
Who can be still until right action is born?

Those who follow this way
and do not desire to be full.

Not seeking to be full,
they can hide and become new

15

The masters of the way
of the creative universe—
back in the old days—knew
the elusive mysteries. Still,

they shuddered like someone
crossing an icy stream;

they stayed awake at night, like
people afraid of their neighbors;

They were serious, like those at
a dinner with powerful people.

They were pliable, like
melting ice; plain, like
unworked wood; cloudy,
like muddy water; empty,
like a mountain gorge.

Muddy water left still a while
will clear; things at rest may
be moved again.

Those who practice
this way of doing
the way stay empty,

looking worn
and unfinished.

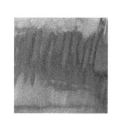

Ah, the ancient masters, they were subtle—
their knowledge was more of a mystery, and was as
deep as it was unfathomable.
Because their wisdom was so impenetrable,

we can only begin to intimate their appearance—
imagining them as standing amid river mists,
crossing the length of an ice-encrusted bridge
in winter.

The ancient masters were as vigilant as anyone who
perceives imminent danger;
as courteous as a conscientious dinner guest;
as yielding as icicles melting from the roof

of a barn;
who offered such simple elegance as an uncut block
of wood;
who were as manifest as clarity is diffused in

an open valley on a cloudless day;
who were as obscured as a mud puddle reflecting sky;
who had the patience for the mud to clear;
who were able to outlast the puddle's murkiness to

become pellucid, again.
Who are those who are able to exercise stillness
until right action emerges to become no action at all?
Disciples of dao are all followers of its way.

They do not actively desire to be enlightened—
and since they do not seek enlightenment,
they sway as they walk while crossing the frozen bridge
over the gorge—

and as ice melts and refreezes—
they have no desire for change.

Empty to the limit, mind still,
ten thousand things combine.
I watch them do it again.
Things grow and grow,
return to their roots.

Return to roots is stillness.
Stillness is return to life.
Return to life is ordinary.

To know the ordinary is to open.
Not to know the ordinary means disaster.
Knowing the ordinary, you will be fair.
Being fair, you will be the best.

The best means heaven.
Heaven means dao.
Dao means long life.

No body, no danger.

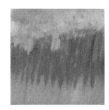

16

To the fullest possible extent, let all thought fall away,
as fresh snow that shifts in the wind.
Allow the mind to become empty in its stillness.

Like so much white among white, in
the moonlit winter darkness, the ten thousand things
swell and fall away, then fuse;

we observe them depart, we see them return.
When things multiply and thrive,
they are returned to their original source.

In returning to their origin, they
are restored to stillness, and are rejoined with nature,
which is the way.

What is unchanging?—the way of nature.
When we come to know the constant of impermanence,
we acquire insight.

When we are not cognizant of this changeless
immutability, it leads to misfortune.
When the ordinary mind is constant, we remain open.

If constraints blocking
the heart are removed, the doors open to its sanctuary.
If there is access to the heart, one's

actions will originate from the source of compassion.
If there is access to compassion, it will lead to divinity—
in harmony with divinity, you become one with dao.

Being at one with dao, you live in the eternity
of the moment. The body passes, falls away, but dao,
this is what always remains.

Cultivate emptiness.
Carefully guard stillness.

All things arise
after their fashion,
then fall to rest again.

Plants grow luxuriant,
then return to their roots,
which is stillness.

That is the unchanging
reality. Knowing this

unchanging reality
is intelligence.

Not knowing it creates
erratic action.

Knowing unchanging reality
creates compassion, and
compassion leads to feeling

one with all.

Feeling one with all
leads to acting in
harmony with all, and
this is the way
of the creative universe.

This way to health; and
when death comes,
there is oneness with all.

What is too high is not known.
Next is what is known and loved,
then what is feared, then
what is despised.

Where belief is lacking,
there is unbelief.

Go slow and value speech.
When work is accomplished,
each and every common
person says
it is I.

17

What is highest is unknown?—
the apotheosis is beyond the reach of man.

Just beneath this, is what we understand
and what and whom we love.

Next, is what is primordial, that surfaces
from the well of fear—

this is what we are only too familiar with.
Ratcheting down the scale, and tightening

the noose in our evolution, is what
is despised, which produces what we fear—

we are all too capable of not only
murdering one, but also of slaughtering many.

For those whom there is
little conception and practice in trusting—

they are not to be trusted.
We need to be scrupulous in what we think—

our thoughts precipitate how we act, and how
we speak, which is of the highest value.

When the work is done, every ordinary person
assumes that it is what they themselves

have achieved, what was accomplished
by each of them individually; whereas, what is

of the highest order transpires only through
the true Self, but still the people insist, "I did it!"

In the early days
people did not know
they had rulers.

Then they noticed
but still had respect.

Next leaders were feared;
then despised.

When leaders do not follow
the way of the creative universe
people do not trust them.

How unsure those ancient
leaders appeared, because
they took their own words seriously.

They achieved what they did
because people said,

"We are doing what we wish."

Abandon the great way,
kindness and justice appear.

Produce wisdom and intelligence,
there is great deceit.

When six relations are not at peace,
there is filial compassion.

When the nation is in chaos,
there are loyal ministers.

18

When following the way fades,
compassion and justice
become techniques.

After that, shrewdness
and hypocrisy
become techniques.

Then relationships lose harmony
and only kinship is important.

Then kinship loses its power and
only paid professionals do the work.

When dao is abandoned,
kindness and justice are popularized, peremptorily.

When kindness and justice pass from
vogue, wisdom and intelligence become the fashion.

This then creates an age from which issues deception.
When social mores crash,

ancestral devotion flourishes—
an interest in referencing genealogy sweeps through

the society, and becomes stylish,
replacing studded leather vests and jade tongue plugs.

When the government is ruled by the deliberate
chaos intended to provide the calculated obfuscation

of both text and subtext to an unwitting populace,
it is generated by the envoys of the oligarchs.

Cut off holiness, abandon wisdom.
The people will profit a hundredfold.

Cut off kindness, abandon justice.
The people will be pious and
compassionate again.

Cut off cleverness, abandon profit.
There will be no thieves.

These three sayings are not enough.

More important is to see the plain,
embrace the simple,
lack selfishness,
have few desires.

19

Forget wisdom;
stop being an expert;
then everybody
is better off.

When we stop
talking about justice,
we will find
honest compassion.

When we drop rhetoric
and forget scheming,
there will be
no more theft.

Three things lead
toward understanding
the way of the universe:

See simply;
act in accord with nature;
forget selfishness.

Then, expectations

disappear.

Renounce religion, step back from intellectual pursuits—
you and everyone else will be better off.

Forego kindness, disavow justice—
you will enter into spirituality, as if you have newly acquired

an ability to walk through walls;
and when you forgive now, out of the heart of compassion,

you will do so without being sanctimonious.
Abjure manipulation, eschew profit—

hooliganism and thievery will be replaced by erecting shrines
hung with wreaths and flowers.

As much as these epigrams
may offer external resolve, they are still not adequate, alone.

You will find it is far more momentous
to observe what is simple; that it is even more consequential,

by being able to see the numinous in the commonplace,
to realize true Self; that in clearly perceiving one's

own fulfillment, we repudiate our selfishness, and in so doing,
mitigate our own more foolish desires.

Cut off learning,
no worries.

Yes and no –
how different are they?

Good and evil –
how different are they?

What people fear,
do not. Do not fear.
How strange!

Everybody prospers as if
they were enjoying a great sacrifice,
as if they were climbing a tower in Spring.
I alone am anchored with no omen,
like an infant not yet a child,
alone as though I had no place to go.

Everybody has more than they need.
I am alone as if abandoned.
I am a fool, confused.

Others are clear and bright.
I alone am dim and faint.
Others are sharp and clever.
I alone am dazed and confused,
like the waves of an ocean endlessly drifting.

Everyone else has a purpose.
I alone am stupid and low.
I am different from others
nourished at my mother's breast.

20

Abandon your studies—
you will then no longer have any concerns about
whether it is *ah* or *oh* or *uh* that you need to use,

and when. But tell me,
is there any difference between yes and no?
How do they differ? Then what about good

and evil? Can you distinguish between them?
And fear—what frightens you, and do you fear
what others fear? Do you find this peculiar?

Most people revel in the providence
of the sacrificial feast. On the first day of spring,
others scale the steps of the pavilion in the park.

But I, not unlike an unmoored boat, drift, aimlessly,
in the current, downstream, beneath the willows.
My eyes, too, roam from one object to another;

and I, too, am like an infant, beginning to learn
the breadth of my smile. Everyone else seems
to have more than enough, but I don't own a thing,

as if I had been abandoned. Apparently, I am
deeply confused—and I act as though I am nothing
but a fool. Others seem to be so glib and quick,

so knowledgeable and keen—while someone is
always finishing my sentences, as I struggle to find
the exact word. I, alone, am muddled, so easily

addled—as in the rolling of ocean waves, I am
pulled farther away from shore, not by the tide
but by the undertow. I, alone, am this elemental,

without purpose—and differ so from all the others.
Especially, since, I have only drawn
sustenance from the breasts of the Great Mother.

Stop seeing distinctions
and there are no worries—
the difference between
"no" and "yes" is so small;

the difference between
good and bad.

Those who fear
are to be feared.

Distinctions:

the multitude enjoy themselves,
as if at a banquet or on a tower
in spring. The Daoist looks
listless and still, nearly invisible.

The Daoist is like a baby
before its first smile,
looking sad, forlorn, homeless.

The multitude appear to have
enough and more. The Daoist—
simple/minded and rumpled—
appears to have nothing at all.

The ordinary look happy,
intelligent; the Daoist looks
benighted.

The ordinary look like
they have all the answers;
the Daoist looks confused,
drifting.

The ordinary have places to be;
the Daoist looks like a bumpkin.

Yes, the Daoist—nourished by
the way of the creative universe
as if it were mother's milk—

is different.

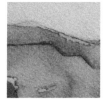

Virtue consists in following dao alone.

As a thing, dao is elusive.
It is elusive.

Within it is an image.
It is elusive.

Within it is content.
It is elusive

Within it is essence.
Its essence is really real.

In it is faith.
From ancient time to now,
its name has not gone away.

Thus the many appear now.
How do we know the state of the many?

Because of this.

21

Following dao, and only dao, accords the highest value.
Unto itself, dao

eludes interpretation—is as indefinable as it is ethereal.
Unto itself, dao is

as impalpable as it is ambiguous; however, image is
within it.

Unto itself, dao is as
evanescent as it is transient; however, form is within it.

Unto itself, dao is
its own distillate of its original manifestation; however,

essence is within it.
Its profound insubstantiality is genuine; whereas, faith

is derived
from it. Its name, since time primordial, to now, never

dissipates or fades.
Creation, exemplified, is exponentially transformative.

How do we know the process of creation perpetuates?
Owing to—*this*.

Those looking for the way
of the creative universe
are willing to keep searching.

Finding the way is difficult,
using sight and touch—the way

cannot be seen or touched,
though it contains all things.

The way eludes sight and touch,
though all events occur there.

All essences, though they are
dark and immaterial, live there.

The life force, though dark
and immaterial, lives there.

The life force does not pass away
and contains everything true.

From today back to the beginning,
the way has been respected.

How has anyone ever known
essences or the life force?

By searching the way!

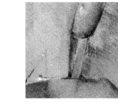

Crooked though whole,
wrong though straight,
sunken though full,
ruined though new,
few though many,
many though puzzled,
so the sage embraces the one.

In order to form the whole world,
not watching oneself,
thus clear
not conceited,
thus distinguished
not boasting,
thus accomplished
not bragging,
thus leading
not fighting.

There is no one in the whole world who fights him.
When the ancients said crooked though whole,
how could that be an empty saying!

Be truly whole,
and all will come to you.

22

Part becomes whole;
crooked, straight;
empty, full;
the wrecked, new.

Those with few desires
get them;
those with many
do not.

For this reason those free
of themselves embrace oneness
and humbleness in the world.

Those free of themselves
are free from egotism.
Therefore, they shine;

they are free from showiness,
therefore are distinguished;

free from bragging,
therefore noticed;
free from self-complacency,
therefore, accomplished.

Because those free
of themselves
do not strive,
no one strives
against them.

In the old days it was said,
"The partial becomes complete."

This is not a vain saying.

Capitulate and triumph; bow and unbend.
Drain and replenish; wear out and renew.

Struggle and prosper; accrue wealth and
be baffled by its conundrum.

Thus, the sage opens to the singularity
of the oneness of everything in the world;

and exemplifies the practice—
of being present moment to moment.

Without self/consciousness,
the sage becomes luminous.

Without condescension, it is the sage
who intrinsically acquires noble attributes.

Without bluster, the sage is acknowledged.
Without bravado, the sage guides.

Since the sage doesn't squabble, no one
disputes what is said.

Thus, the immemorial ones counsel:
"Capitulate and triumph."

Then how could this be a vacuous phrase?
Be absolute

in accepting all as one; being whole,
everything that transpires will be as it should.

Infrequent speech is natural.
A gale doesn't last all morning.
A squall doesn't last all day.

Why is this? Heaven and earth.
If heaven and earth are not eternal,
how could a human being be?

On the way, be one with the way.
Succeeding, be one with success.
Failing, be one with failure.

One with the way,
the way is happy.
One with success,
success is happy.
Losing, lose happily.

Not trusting enough,
not trusted.

23

By nature we speak few words—
after all, high winds don't last all morning;
a downpour does not fall all day.

Why? Because even the earth,
even the sky, can't stay violent long.

When we study the way
of the creative universe,
those pursuing it agree with us,
and those practicing it agree with us,
and even those failing to live up to
their aspirations agree with us.

When we study the way,
those attempting to practice it
agree with us, and those attempting
to pursue it agree with us, and
even those who don't even try

agree with us.

But when we stop
our own attempts,
everyone loses faith.

To be reticent in speech exercises prudence.
After all, does a gale blow for an entire
morning? Don't the gusts of a squall, that

by definition are transitory outbursts
of weather, only last for less than a day?
As a child may ask a question, "Is there an

answer?" Heaven and earth. If what is
ephemeral, in heaven and on earth, then
how could the same not be true for mortal

humans? Whereas, anyone who imitates
the way eventually becomes one with dao.
Furthermore, anyone who succeeds in

following the way becomes one with
the virtue of dao. Although, anyone who
loses the way becomes as lost as on the trail

beneath the pines that obscure the light
of the moon. When anyone is at one with
the way, dao greets that person in felicity.

When anyone is at one with the virtue of dao,
that individual will succeed in always finding
the way. When it is necessary to become

one with loss, it is wise to value that, and to
embrace loss as a trusted friend.
Whereas, for anyone who has not sufficiently

trusted, such as this, they will find
no one, whatsoever, who will ever be fully
confident to depend on them for anything.

One who tiptoes doesn't stand.
One who strides doesn't walk.
One who is self-conscious doesn't know.
One who is conceited is not seen.
One who flatters himself accomplishes nothing.
One who boasts does not endure.

One who is on the road says
that is extra food and
excess baggage.

Some things are evil.
One on the road has no place for them.

24

One who tiptoes is unsteady.
One who overstrides never finds a rhythm

with such an unstable gait.
One who gives way to ostentation deviates

from the path to enlightenment.
One who is narcissistic will never lack in

having at least one admirer, but will have no
real acquaintances or true friends.

One who blusters and rants
wears out any listener, and is en route

to accomplishing less than nothing.
For anyone who is a traveler on the way

of dao—
this is a glutton's serving of food

and an excess of unwieldy encumbrances.
They have no merit; and they drive foment

and dispense malaise.
Anyone traveling the way of dao needs to

not only evade
such depraved notions, but to also find it

necessary to free themselves
from any such obstacles to consciousness.

Those who stand on tiptoes
do not stand firm.
Those with long strides
do not walk comfortably.
Those with loud opinions
are not heard.
Those showing off
do not shine.

No one sees the conceited as
worthy.
From the point of view of the way
all the above are like
crumbs on the face or

sores that no one wants to see.

Those who pursue the way
do not do these things.

There is something nebulous
born before the world
in silence and emptiness.

Standing alone and changeless,
it walks everywhere and is not in danger.

It could be the mother of the whole world.
I do not know its name.
Call it dao.

Forced to name it,
I call it great.

Great means flow,
flow means far,
far means return.

Dao is great.
Heaven is great.
Earth is great.
The people are also great.

These are the four powers,
and the people are one of them.

The people follow earth,
earth follows heaven,
heaven follows dao,
dao follows nature.

25

Something undefined and complete,
existed before the earth and sky.

It was formless, still, alone, changeless.
It extended everywhere without effort—
is is the mother of all things.

I do not know its name,
but I call it the way
of the creative universe—
even The Great Way.

Great, it flows on.
Passing, it is distant.
Having become distant,
it draws near again.

The way is great;
the sky is great;
the earth is great;
a wise leader is great.

We humans take our laws from the earth;
the earth takes its laws from the sky;
the sky takes its laws from the way;
the law of the way is being as such.

Something exists
that is more amorphous than water.
In the soundless hush of the void,
it predates the world—

solitary and timelessly constant;
fluidly in motion and never in peril—
this, perhaps, is what is known as
the mother of the ten thousand things.

Refer to it as you wish, call it dao;
with respect to myself, it lures me, but
I am unsure of what its name is.
Because I believe in the significance of

names, I call it the spectral resplendent.
Resplendent means to pour forth,
spectral indicates being otherworldly.
To pour forth suggests not only

resilience but also distance.
Distance intimates return, to return
infers reciprocity; offering reciprocity
it is fluidly in motion and pours forth.

Consequently, dao is fluid and spills
like a gold and silver ribbon from
the mountain cliffs in the sunlight—
blessing the earth, as it pours and

froths over the stones, which inspires
those who experience this grace.
Of the four powers, the spectral
resplendent is one of them, which

we are drawn to, and follow—
as the gold and silver ribbon pours
from the mountain cliffs, even just
the sound issuing from its roar

is a praise to the earth. In this, what
is ephemeral is made palpable; and its
presence arises from the otherworldly—
which is what emanates from dao.

Heavy is the root of light.
Still is ruler of impatient.

Thus a noble who travels all day
does not stray far from his baggage.

Though there are glories to see,
he does not get carried away.

Why should the master of the whole world
carry himself light as the world?

Too light is to lose one's root.
Too impatient is to lose control.

26

Heaviness is the root of lightness;
stillness determines movement.

The wise, traveling all day,
never stray far from supplies.
Only close to home can we relax.

Do the wise take
their bodies lightly?

To do so is to forget the root,
to get lost in movement,

forgetting the goal.

In balance, and in opposition—
what is weighty is the root, and ballast,

to what is ethereal, and what rises.
What masters impatience, with its

trotting imperatives, is the stillness when
the wind

stops blowing across the open meadow.
In keeping with the tenants of wisdom,

while traveling,
the sage does not abandon his trunks

when stopping to view the mist rise from
the snowcapped mountains.

One abides by becoming as unattached as
the mountains are to the mist—

by letting go, as the wisps
dissolve in the air. Why should an adept

of the ten thousand things prefer
to adopt a deportment of moderation?

To move easily among people, and their
own predilections,

it is best
to lose the root of heaviness.

To lose one's itching restlessness is to be
at ease in the world.

Good walk, no tracks.
Good talk, no disgrace.
Good reckoning, no tally.
Good closing, no lock –
yet no one can open it.
Good tying, no knot –
yet no one can loosen it.

So the sage is good at saving lives
and abandons no one,
is good at saving things
and abandons nothing.

This is called inheriting light.

A good person is a bad person's teacher.
A bad person is a good person's wealth.
Not honoring his teacher,
not honoring his wealth –
great confusion though wise.

This is called essential mystery.

27

One who walks mindfully leaves no tracks.
One who speaks clearly doesn't stumble.
One who settles their accounts
frees themselves of endless calculations.

A well-made door exhibits how skillfully
it is crafted
by how easily one can pass through it
and if anyone is able to open it

after it is locked.
The binding that doesn't entail tying knots
is the one that is impossible to untangle.
Similarly, the sage is attentive

to everyone, and indifferent to no one.
In tending to all things,
not one is renounced or deserted.
What is this path called?

It is known as the one of *inherent light.*
What constitutes goodness in anyone?—
being able to teach someone who is
corrupt; and what is it that constitutes

anyone of such wrongdoing?—
by having willfully deviated against nature.
If the teacher is not given respect, and
if the student is not shown attentiveness,

disorder will abound, no matter what
ingenuity is used—
getting to the core of this is the point
in resolving what is a true paradox.

Skillful travelers leave no trace,
neither of wheel nor footstep.

Skillful speakers make no remarks,
spreading neither fault nor blame.

Skillful mathematicians need no calculators.
Skillful carpenters need neither bolt nor bar,

yet what they shut no one opens.

Skillful binders use no strings or knots,
yet untying their work is impossible.

Those free of their themselves ignore nothing.
Those free of themselves waste nothing.
Those free of themselves use innate skill.

Others may learn from this.

Respecting the skillful and gaining
respect from the skillful opens
the way to learning mysteries.

Know the masculine,
preserve the feminine.

Be the stream of the world.
Be the stream of the world.

Common virtue, not rare –
become a child again.
Know the white,
preserve the black.

Be the rule of the world.
Be the rule of the world.

Common virtue, not excessive –
become limitless again.
Know honor,
preserve humility.

Be the valley of the world.
Be the valley of the world.

Common virtue suffices.
Become plain again.
Be the rule of the world.

A block of wood carved becomes a vessel.
The sage uses it as his highest minister.

The master tailor does not cut.

28

Know the masculine
and the feminine.

In that knowledge become
a flowing stream, strong,
full, coursing through
all humanity, just like
a newborn babe.

Know the pure;
value the impure,

and so become a valley
strong and full,
like unworked wood.

Know the light;
value the dark,

and so become an example,
strong and full, containing
the human, yet
becoming boundless.

When unworked wood
is worked, it becomes
many things.

When those free of themselves
are worked, they become wise.

In the best working,
there is no sharpness.

Be cognizant of masculine mythology.
Be mindful of the mythological feminine.
Become the torrent of the universe—
being the surge outpouring into the world,

you will become steadfast and unwavering;
in so doing, you will see, again, as through
the eyes of a child, into the depths of things,
viewing them as if for the first time.

Be attentive of the white keys—
however, be au fait of what is contributed
in playing the black keys, either alone,
or in harmony with the white ones.

Be the paradigm of the world—
in being such an exemplar you provide
a sign in guiding others along the way.
Look within, perceive your limitlessness.

Be observant in regarding the esteem
of others—
know how to maintain your own humility,
through the practice of putting others

first. Become the valley of the world—
in being the basin of the universe,
you will become devoted to creativity,
and all things will work through you.

Be sure to allow yourself to be restored
to your true origins—
as a block of wood is before it is carved
to make a vessel.

Use it wisely after it is fashioned, as if it
were being used by a sage, in moderation,
allowing the sage to become an adept
on the way—

in keeping with a master tailor who can be
heard using the scissors only once in a while.

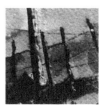

Do you wish to take over
and govern the whole world?

I don't see this succeeding.
The whole world is sacred.

It can't be governed.
It can't be held.

You will spoil it.
To hold it is to lose it.

Sometimes things lead,
sometimes things follow.

Sometimes praise, sometimes boast,
sometimes strong, sometimes weak,
sometimes carry, sometimes overthrow.

The sage avoids extremes,
avoids extravagance,
avoids exaltation.

29

Do you believe you can expropriate
the world, as a landlord exercises the clauses
in a contract to takeover buildings,
housing small businesses, in order to renovate

them for luxury apartments in town?
The attempt can be made; however,
the enormity of the world is of a magnitude
beyond even the extent of barbarous avarice.

Since the expanse of the world is sacred,
no one person can be its sovereign.
The whole world is of such a scale that
no one can quite grasp it—

nor can it be bent to serve,
in any other way than it already is, naturally.
If you attempt to possess the world,
your greed will impoverish it.

There are some things that point the way;
sometimes they come after.
Sometimes, one bows in reverence; other
times, instead of venerating what is valued,

one finds occasion to make heedless boasts.
There are times when we surprise ourselves,
and others, by our uncanny strength—
in various circumstances,

disappointing those we love distresses us.
Sometimes, one sustains the weight
of expectations; other times we are toppled
by our own inchoate conjectures.

It is significant to observe what the sage avoids:
any level of antipodal digressions,
spates of self-indulgent embellishments,
even just a modicum of smug rapture.

Try to seize a nation
and so discover failure.

Nations are living things,
so cannot be got by grasping.

Those who attempt
to conquer will destroy.
Those who grasp will
find nothing to hold.

It is the way of the creative
universe that front becomes
back; warm turns to freezing,
strong becomes weak;
storehouses empty out.

Thus it is that those free
of themselves relax—

forgetting extravagance;
forgetting striving.

Use dao to assist a ruler.
Don't use weapons to conquer the world.
This is to serve well.

Master a place,
thorn bushes spring up.
After armies pass there must be a difficult year.

Get good results, that's all.
Don't dare seek power.

Get results, don't dwell on them.
Get results, don't cut down.
Get results, don't be arrogant.
Get results when there is no alternative.
Get results, don't struggle.

Strength grows old.
This is not the way.
What is not the way ends early.

30

Advocate to those who govern to follow dao.
Convince them that using weapons
to seize control of the world only increases
opposition, becomes an agent of resistance.

Once land is overtaken in battle,
nettles and briars emerge from the blood and
ashes, after armies, by turns,
have advanced and retreated.

Following the conflict of war, what is forged
are the links in the chain that become
a concatenation of grim years.
Real wisdom, simply, is attending to what is

necessary that gets things done—
to take advantage of power causes
contemptible repercussions and reprehensible
aftershocks.

Nourish outcomes, but never seek acclaim.
Work toward solutions that culminate
in mutual benefit to all, but never vaunt
your success.

Realize the consequences of your best actions,
but refrain from extolling them.
Get things done—
our instinct knows no other healthy alternative.

For the best results, they are never achieved
through brute force.
Intimidation and violence conclude in injury
and loss. None of this is conduct appropriate

to practicing the way.
Such inconsistencies run contrary to the grain
in the wood and weakens its structure,
so that it fractures easily.

What offers such resistance to dao induces its
own untimely end.

Here is advice for leadership
in the way
of the creative universe:

do not look to force—
the result is predictable.

Wherever an army is,
briars and thorns spring up.

Large armies lead to hunger.

A skillful commander strikes
a decisive blow, never seeking
total victory. He will win, then
guard against his own arrogance.

He strikes because he must,
with no thought of victory.

Nothing comes to fruition
before its time, which is
the way of the way.

What is not in accord dies.

Weapons are inauspicious tools, all despise them.
So those who follow the dao do not use them

31

The noble person honors the left.
The warrior honors the right.

Weapons are inauspicious tools.
The noble person does not use them
unless there is no alternative.
Peace and quiet are best.

Victory is not beautiful.
Beautify it, and you are happy with murder.
One who is happy with murder
achieves no worldly rule.

We honor the left as a good omen,
the right as ominous.

The general stands on the left,
the commander in chief on the right—
as at a funeral.

When many people are killed,
they should be mourned.

When a victory is won,
treat it as a funeral.

Weapons are tools that yield unpropitious results.
They are abhorrent—
representing the negative numbers of overriding joy.
Those who are devotees of the way never use them.

Those who are wise favor the left.
Those who promote war choose the right.
What produces the most unpropitious results are
weapons that are used as tools.

Those who are virtuous never exploit weapons,
unless they are unable to choose another option.
For such a person, what is simple and unadorned,
and what is undisturbed and unobtrusive, are valued.

There is no delight to be found in annihilation—
it is repugnant.
Manslaughter is no motive for jubilation.
For those who find any allure in carnage

will never find the universe within.
On the occasion of what is auspicious, we honor
the left. In the event of inexpressible sorrow,
and what is ominous,

one's foreboding of death haunts us on the right.
The army general endures the battlefield on the left.
The commander-in-chief issues orders for caskets
on the right.

The obsequies should be declared in boot camp,
even before basic training begins.
When any number of
people are murdered in the name of *a good war,* we

should mourn for those whose icy absence chills
us all.
That is why we should think of triumph as paying
our respects at a funeral.

Weapons are instruments of death.
Therefore, living things hate them.

Followers of the way
of the creative universe
avoid weapons except in
necessity, preferring calm.

Avoid victory by force;

violence leads
only to violence.

Remember: a killer
is never prized long.

Celebrate a victory
like a funeral.

Common dao has no name.
Though simple and small,
none can grasp it.

If nobles and kings could harness it,
the whole world would naturally be their guest.

Heaven and earth would embrace,
and sweet dew would settle.

The people would need no more orders,
since all would follow their natural course.

A system begins, and there are names.
Since there are already names,

we should know when to stop.
If we know when to stop,
we are in no danger.

An example of dao in the world
is a river in a valley flowing down to the sea.

32

The unchanging way remains undefined.
Even though it is small and simple,
no one dares claim to be its master.

If leaders really mastered it,
all would submit to them—the sky
and earth would suddenly unite,

raining down plenty, and
all people would share,
fairly, without compulsion.

When the way of the creative
universe becomes action,
we have a name for that action.

When we have a name for it,
all people see it is correct,
without any effort at knowing.

Our reality is related to the way,
just as rivers are to the sea.

The definition of dao has no borders.
No one can comprehend it, although dao is

unadorned, infinitesimal.
If those who govern could access it, it would

be as if it were their visitant, giving them counsel
to the ten thousand things—

both heaven and earth would comply with such
an arrangement—

as the dew that forms its droplets, coating
the lushness of the grass on a summer morning.

The people would no more need guidance—
it would follow that harmony would

find a groove, and become actively intuitive.
Once you institute a system, which, even

inadvertently, separates what is of this world,
everything, then, needs to be named.

Already enough, there are too many names.
One exercises prudence in knowing when

to cease any activity.
Observing when it is timely to stop affords us

no harm. What is exemplary of dao
moving through this world is the sinuousness

of a river undulating, in all
of its radiance, to the glistening body of the sea.

One who knows people is wise.
One who knows oneself is enlightened.
One who conquers people is powerful.
One who conquers oneself is strong.
One who knows enough is rich.
One who strives is willful.
One who does not lose his place endures.
One who dies but does not perish lives long.

33

Those who know
the other
have learning.

Those who know
themselves
have wisdom.

Those who overcome
others
have strength.

Those who overcome
themselves
have power.

Those who know
enough is enough
are rich.

Those with resolve
go on.

Those with hope
go on and on.

Those who die
yet are not
forgotten

live.

Those who perceive others are sagacious.
Those who practice self-discernment

are on the way to experiencing the many
loops in the trail, that recross themselves,

up the mountain, toward just the beginning
of enlightenment, at the crest of the summit.

Those who endeavor on
the path awaken the consciousness within.

Those who tend to finding the center
persist in their replenishment by abiding

in the immovable spot. To pass from this
life, but to become one of the immortals,

is to be permanently present—
streaming, in the current, always *here,*

in living
in the *now,* perpetuating one's existence—

infinite moment,
arising and falling away, to eternal moment.

Great dao floods.
It may go left or right.

All beings rely on it
to give life and not take leave.

34

It does its work but has no reputation.
It gives birth to all beings but is not their master.

It has no desire.
It may be called small.

All beings return to it,
but it is not their master.

It may be called big.
Because it does not act great,
it can do great things.

The essence
of the way
is left,
is right,
is all around.

It gives all,
takes nothing.

It accomplishes all,
claims nothing.

It clothes all,
feeds all, yet
seeks no
power.

There it is, one
of the smallest
of things.

Because it
has power over
everything yet
claims no power,
it is the most
powerful thing.

Those free of themselves
may learn from this:

power comes
from…

not seeking power.

The cascading flux of dao rushes everywhere—
it courses both to the left and to the right.

All beings and the ten thousand things find
nourishment and guidance from it—

when it is impeded, dao surges around whatever
blocks it, as the rushing of a brook, whose

rivulets runnel around the stones in its current.
It is the source of the ten thousand things.

It is similar to a monk in a hermitage, who
is engaged in doing the real work, who sweats

in the splitting and the stacking of the wood,
but takes no credit in performing the labor.

Through its unimaginable magnitude of small
ways, it exhibits its true largesse.

The ten thousand things emerge from it, and
they return to it.

Although it may be assumed to
possess enormity, its size is not of significance—

simply, because
it actually offers such eminent consequences.

Because it does not aspire to greatness—
IT IS.

35

Hold up a great image,
and the whole world will come.

Be beyond harm,
quiet and peaceful,
with music and good food.
Passing guests will stop.

When dao speaks,
it is insipid and tasteless.

We look and don't see,
listen and don't hear.

But its usefulness is never exhausted.

Write the character for anyone who keeps to the way
and those who seek the same path

will flock to whoever this person may be—
if only for the unconscious necessity to

experience the electric synchronicity of being filled
with finding the transcendent in the commonplace.

All those who pass by, unknowingly, will be drawn
to this person,

as they are to euphonious music or fine cuisine.
However, when someone describes dao,

it is as if they are representing something that is
discordant and bland.

This dao that we speak of, that we look for but can't
see, and that we listen for but can't hear—

what a thing it is, whose inestimable merit is so
plentiful that it is limitless.

Take hold of the larger vision
and let the world come to you—

no harm, only rest and peace.

Music and fine food
stop travelers, while
the way appears dull—

nothing to hear,
nothing to taste.

Yet the flavors
of the way
are endless.

What you wish to contract
you must first expand.

What you wish to weaken
you must strengthen.

What you wish to give up
you must relish.

What you wish to take
you must give.
This is called trifling light.

Soft defeats hard,
weak defeats strong.

Fish can't escape the deep.
A nation's greatest tool
may not be shown.

36

A breath out
implies
a breath in.

Weakening implies
gaining strength.

What is torn down
first must be
raised up.

Whatever is taken
must have been
available.

This is the subtlety
in the obvious.

The soft—the weak—
overcomes the strong.

Fish thrive in the depths.

Nations thrive by keeping
their strengths hidden.

Whatever that is diminished
is something that had already been amplified.

Whatever founders, then fails, flourished once,
and was vital.

Whatever you are forced to relinquish,
or abdicate, you first must savor, or elevate.

Whatever you desire to possess, or to
magnanimously accept, as a gift, you will need

to initially renounce, and then to bestow.
This is known as the awareness

of the inconsequential essence of all things—
what is subdued and compliant

transcends what is forceful and unyielding.
The fish in the sea

are unable to avoid swimming in deep water.
Any nation's greatest asset

is to resist making an ostentatious exhibition
of the weaponry in their arsenal.

Dao does nothing,
and yet there is nothing
it does not do.

If nobles and kings could harness it,
all beings would change naturally.

And if change gave rise to desire
they would be composed with unknown
simplicity. Composed with unknown simplicity,

they would not desire.
Desireless, at peace,
the whole world
would make itself whole.

37

Dao manifests by non-action.
It reveals nothing since there is nothing

for it to reveal.
If those who govern could abide by this,

all would progress within its nature and
prosper.

Even if they were to keep choosing action
over non-action, they could still benefit

by the practice of finding the numinous
in the commonplace.

Within what is formless, desire does not
exist.

Without desire, if harmony were
to have a melody, such a music would be

stillness.
Therefore, what is absolute in the world

would be complete, and would become
whole, in its entirety.

The way of the creative
universe has no labels.

If we all could remember this,
all would go by nature. Then,
anytime we forgot, simplicity
would be a sufficient reminder.

Simplicity would remind and
we could stop reaching.

Without reaching we could
find the un-named. And

the world would
find its order.

德
DE

Higher virtue is not virtuous, so it has virtue.
Lower virtue never fails to be virtuous, so it has no virtue.

Higher virtue does nothing
for the sake of something else,
and nothing is for the sake of something else.

Lower virtue does nothing
for the sake of something else,
and is for the sake of something else.

Higher kindness is for something, and nothing is done.
Higher justice is for something, and there is something to do.

Higher propriety is for something, and there is no ought.
It takes law up and lays it down.

When dao gets old and lost, there is virtue.
When virtue is lost, there is kindness.
When kindness is lost, there is justice.
When justice is lost, there is propriety.

The proper person is one
whose belief is waning
and getting confused.

Prophecy is a flashy dao
starting to get stupid.

True greatness is thick, not thin,
real, not flash. Let that go to get this.

38

For someone who is good, that person is not aware
of goodness; therefore, that is an indication that he is good.
For someone who is foolish, whatever he may do never
leads to goodness; consequently, he is not good.

Someone, who is good, does not need to do anything.
Someone, who is a fool, is always doing something;
but, in what he does, he always leaves so much more to do.
When someone, who is profoundly kind, does something,

that person leaves nothing that is unfinished.
When someone, who is equitable, does something,
that person always leaves much left to accomplish.
When someone, who is an authoritarian, does anything,

there is not one person who wants to respond—
the authoritarian gets ready to go to work with a dusting
off of his hands, then attempts to enlist others to do
the work for him.

So, when dao is missing and forgotten, there is goodness.
When goodness is missing and forgotten what remains is
kindness.
When kindness is missing and forgotten, what replaces it

is justice.
When justice is missing and forgotten, what takes its place
is ceremony without the insight
of myth, which becomes the emptiness of protocol.

What protocol generates are the germs of belief and faith,
which herald the beginning of the age of confusion.
Prescience is just the ostentation of someone who is
ensnared in the misunderstanding of dao.

So, one who is an adept, that person focuses on what is
genuine, and not what is superficial—
on the yield and not the bloom.
We need to nourish one and to relinquish the other.

The wise do not strive
and are therefore effective.

The lackluster never stop striving,
and therefore achieve little.

The wise never force, knowing
force gets nothing done.

The wise bring compassion because
they aren't thinking about it.

The wise create justice because
they don't worry about it.

Those concerned with appearances
have good reason to coerce others.

Those concerned
only with ritual
must use brute force.

So, only in not striving
are we followers of the way;

only in not forcing
do we lead appropriately;

only in not coercing do
we encourage ritual.

Ritual is, after all,
only a show
of commitment;

a pretense toward the way
of the creative universe
and a foolish one at that.

This is why the wise pay
attention to the real,

keeping watch on the fruit,
not the flower—leaving

the one, taking the other.

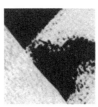

That which became one in the beginning –
Sky became one to be clear.
Earth became one to be peaceful.
Spirit became one to be agile.
Grain became one to be full.
The universe became one to be alive.
Nobles and kings became one
to make the whole world upright.

This also means that sky that is not to be
clear is broken, earth that is not to be
peaceful is wasted, spirit that is not to be
agile is still, grain that is not to be full is exhausted.

A universe that is not to be alive is extinguished.
Kings and nobles that are not to be loyal will fall.

What is honored is rooted in what is lowly.
The high is founded on what is basic.

Thus nobles and kings call themselves
orphaned, widowed, destitute.

Is this not the basis of humility?
to be interested in reputation
is to have no reputation.

Don't jingle like jade,
like a necklace of stones.

39

Some things
have known
the way from
the beginning—

the sky in its clarity;
the earth in its solidity;
the spirit in its vitality;
the valleys in their fullness.

The wise ones who have realized
the oneness of existence.

All these result from watching
the way of the creative universe.

If the sky had not found clarity
would it not have fallen to pieces?

If the earth had not found solidity
would it not have collapsed?

If the spirit had not found vitality
would it ever have gotten lively?

If the valleys had not found fullness
would they not have dried up?

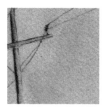

If some wise ones had not realized
the oneness of life wouldn't all be chaos?

Complexity requires simple roots;
loftiness requires a firm foundation;

This is why wise ones call themselves
lonely;
inept.
By so saying,
they acknowledge the humbleness
of human roots.

The greatest dignity
is to feel no dignity;

to be as precious as jade we
must be as common as stone.

Emerging from its origin of what is whole—
sky merged with what is one to become lucent and cerulean;
earth united with what is one to become undisturbed and
solid ground;

spirit coalesced with what is one to become lithe and supple;
fields of grain, in the valley, fused with what is one
to become abundant and yielding;
the cosmos conjoined its constellations with what is one for

the singular purpose of being and to become divine nature;
those who govern combined with what is one to pledge to
uphold what is principled and to make their populace compliant.
What all of this means is all of that—CARDINAL VIRTUE.

What is lucent and cerulean about
the sky insures its not becoming opaque and turning black.
What is undisturbed and solid about the earth forestalls its
rampant contamination.

What is lithe and supple about the spirit
prevents it from becoming impoverished and exhausting itself.
What is abundant and yielding about the valley of grain
saturates and sustains it from becoming desiccated and withered.

Even those who govern normally attempt to serve the purpose
of preventing the country from coming undone and chaos ensuring.
What is esteemed finds its origin in what is disreputable.
What is dishonorable acquires its reputation by what is virtuous.

Those who work for those who govern often think
of themselves as: ESTRANGED, INDIGENT, BEREFT.
Those who value their reputation do not concern themselves
with needing to preserve it. For a teacher to include too much

knowledge in a lecture, it is not only unwise but also lacking
in humility. The best practice encourages us not to jangle like
the clattering of jade bracelets, or to collide in a tintinnabulation—
as do the strings of stones in a set of wind chimes.

Dao moves the other way.
Dao uses weakness.

Everything in the whole world
is born of something.

Something is
born of nothing.

40

The way of the
creative universe
moves
in circles—
in spirals.

Through weakness,
the way is mighty.

Everything under the sky;
all of existence
in all its names—

sprang to being from
this absence,

this unnamed.

Dao is in the motion of eternal yield and return.
The way of dao is capitulation—
its cycle begets and nourishes the process of creation.

What is absolute is that all things are kindled into
being, along the wheel of birth, from non-being, out of
their original essence and quiddity.

Even before the point of what emerges
from its nascency, and it is born into being, it originates
from what had previously not existed at all.

41

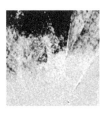

The wise scholar hears the dao and walks it diligently.
The average scholar hears the dao and can take it or leave it.
The poor scholar hears the dao and laughs out loud.

If there were no laughter.
dao would not be what it is.

Therefore it is said
the bright path appears dark,
the way forward appears to be the way back,
the easy way appears hard,
the highest virtue appears to be a valley,
the greatest purity appears to be a disgrace,
the most vast virtue appears to be stolen,
the most real substance appears to be changing,
the perfect square has no corners,
great talent ripens slowly,
great sound is muted,
the highest image has no shape.

Dao is hidden and nameless.
Only dao nourishes and fulfills.

The discriminating student listens to dao and is
immersed in its flow.
The ordinary student hears dao and throws up
his hands in apathetic indifference.

The doltish student
catches just a phrase of dao and chuckles audibly.
Accordingly, various aphorisms include:
the sunlit path is often darkest at the trailhead

beneath the trees; frequently,
going forward on the trail to the summit seems
as if we were stepping in place;
in facilitating the easiest choices always presents

the most obstinate difficulties;
choosing what is of the highest virtue apparently
leads us through a valley of the darkest inequity;
practicing diligence sometimes

yields insufficient results;
in cases of exhibiting ethical rectitude we may be
besmirched and tainted;
in regard to exercising the characteristics that apply

to what is virtuous, it often requires us to persevere
through purported accusations that lay fault to
and blemish our own reputation;
what is perfect about what is square is that it has

no corners;
the development of genius insures that there are no
overnight successes;
commonly, the most harmonious music is performed

softly; what materializes as significant in appearance
is usually shapeless.
Dao is inscrutable and inviolate—it is nameless.
Simply, dao, singularly, fosters the fulfillment of all.

Serious students find
a way and

practice it diligently.

Those less serious
sometimes practice
and sometimes don't.

Those less serious still
merely laugh at any way—

which proves this is serious.

Ancient writers said
this of the way of
the creative universe:

At its brightest,
the way looks dark.

Those following it
appear to be
going backward.

Its smoothest places
are a rugged path;

its highest places
look like a valley.

Its greatest beauty
offends the eyes.

Those with most
appear to have least.

The excellence of the way
looks lax; the solidest
truth looks like sand;

the perfect square
has no corners;
its loudest sound
makes no noise at all.

It is amorphous,
unfinished.

It is the shadow
of a shadow.

The way is hidden,
is nameless; the way

is the beginning that
finishes everything.

Dao gives birth to one. One
gives birth to two. Two
gives birth to three. Three
gives birth to ten thousand things.

Ten thousand things carry yin and embrace yang.
By means of these forces they achieve harmony.

People hate to be orphaned, widowed, destitute –
but this is what public officials call themselves.

Thus by losing one gains,
by gaining one loses.

What is taught by others, I teach too.
The powerful do not choose death.

This will be the father of my teaching.

42

One originates in the way
of the creative universe;

that one produces two;
two produces three;

three produces all that is.

All things leave behind
the obscurity from whence
they come, moving to
embrace the brightness

into which they go,
harmonizing in
the breath of the void.

We wish for friends;
wish for achievement;
long for a place.

Leaders cannot have friends,
achievement, or place.

Some things lose by increasing;
others increase by losing.

What many have taught,
I also teach:

the strong
and violent
do not die
naturally.

This is the center
of the teachings.

Dao yields one.
  From one arises two.
    Two nurtures three.

Three precipitates
  what is exponential—
    the ten thousand things.

The ten thousand things
  guide the fluidity of ying,
    sustain the power of yang.

Through the alchemy
  of the gyre of their perpetuity,
    they combine to create

the universal symmetry
  that is represented
    in the symbol of taijitu—

image of the absolute.
  People abhor losing
    one's parents; or in

experiencing the death
  of a spouse; or when they
    become indigent for being

fired from a job.
  However, those who govern
    identify themselves as such.

Therefore, one enjoys favorable
  gains in such trenchant loses.
    Thus, by such significant

gains, one is pierced with
  loss, as if by a long spear.
    What previous teachers

have taught,
  I also give parallel
    instruction: those who

wish to be masters
  of themselves,
    do not achieve control

through violent acts;
  incontrovertibly, this
    is not only the basis

of my teaching,
  but it is also
    the resin from which

the incense is derived
  that provides the aromatic
    redolence of its essence.

The softest thing in the whole world
dominates the hardest thing
in the whole world.

Nothing enters no room, so I know
nothing for nothing else is beneficial.

Teaching without speaking,
the benefit of nothing
for nothing else

is rarely achieved in the whole world.

43

This, out of the whole world, is what is the single
element that influences and

sways what is resistant—it is what is most pliant,
in this whole world.

This is of such immateriality that it suffuses any
space,

even in which there is not any more room for it
to fill.

Therefore, I am not aware of anything else
that possesses any more value than by doing by

non-action.
Such is the benefit of teaching

without making use of
words, and working by not doing anything at all.

How infrequently
this is comprehended in the whole world—

AH, only by a smattering, a bare modicum, just by
a rare few.

The softest thing may
crush the hardest;

only the insubstantial
can penetrate the solid—

this is how we know
the way of never forcing
is the most effective way.

Only a few can follow
a teaching beyond words;

only a few can follow
a way that never pushes.

Name or life – which matters?
Life or possessions – which?
Gain or loss – which is the disease?

Great love means great expense.
Much saved means much lost.

One who knows what will suffice
will not be humiliated.

One who knows when to stop
will not be in danger
and will endure.

44

Your money or your life—
which is worth more to you?

Reputation or life—which
is more important to you?

Lose your possessions;
lose your life—

which brings more
sorrow and pain?

Clinging to reputation means
letting go of what is important.

Clutching at possessions means
letting go of greater riches.

Contentment finds no shame;
discretion finds no dishonor;

follow these and live long.
Identity or soul—
of which of these matters most?

Identity or soul—
of which of these matters most?
Our very existence
or our treasured belongings—
of these which?

And between our amassing
profit, then accruing debt—
of which affliction are we more
disposed to?
The one who loves deeply will

suffer from an eternal ache.
The one who conserves and tends
to the tradition of husbandry
approaches life on the earth in
honoring it and not squandering it.

The one who basks
in self/satisfaction is mollified
by the grace of sheer delight.
The one who practices active
understanding exercises prudence

in accommodating for what is
just enough, and will circumvent
the disgrace of scandal.
This one will remain steadfast
and unfaltering in any event of peril.

Great achievement seems lacking,
but its use is not wrong.

Great fulfillment seems washed out,
but its use is not exhausted.

Great straightness seems bent.
Great skillfulness seems clumsy.
Great debate seems to stammer.

Stillness overcomes impatience.
Cold overcomes heat.

Quiet tranquility
makes the whole world right.

45

Seen from the way
of the creative universe,
the most thoroughly completed
looks like so many pieces.

Use it and use it.
Its fullness looks
like a hole—

the straightest looks crooked;
the most graceful looks clumsy;
eloquence sounds like stuttering.

Motion beats the cold;
stillness beats the heat.

Peace and serenity
run the universe.

Considerable attainment appears less than perfect;
however, its relevance endures.

Substantial consummation, after following the way,
can leave one spent

and haggard, but its benefits are not to be exhausted.
The vertical rise often doesn't show plumb.

The adept reach, or thought, sometimes looks clumsy,
or although cogent, is initially inchoate.

Creative expression may sound grossly inarticulate.
To keep warm in the cold practice movement.

To abate the heat— it is wise to stop, to rest, to stay
still.

Calmness and peacefulness harmonize to engender
serenity in the world.

When the whole world is dao,
horses manure fields.

When the whole world is not dao,
war horses are born on the border.

No disaster is greater than desire,
no curse greater than getting what you desire.

To know what will suffice is to be finally satisfied.

46

When the way is followed,
horses plow the fields;

when it is not followed,
horses storm cities.

Greed is the greatest crime;
wanting more,
the greatest tragedy.

Know what is enough
and be content.

When you see dao active in the world,
work horses strain against their harness

to pull the manure wagons through the fields.
When you see that dao is inactive in the world,

be sure that war horses procreate and are born,
on the frontier, beyond the walled city—

neighing, biting each other, and imperiously
stamping their hooves.

There is nothing more tragic than
people who implacably demand to have their

own way, or no way at all.
There is no malediction more severe

than to suffer the indignity of obtaining what
you desire.

To become aware of what will do, of what will
serve, and what is

irrevocably enough—
that inner knowledge of what is adequate

will provide anyone ample
gratification and an abundance of contentment.

Without going out the door,
know the whole world.

Without watching
out the window,
see everyday dao.

The farther you go, the less you know.
the sage does not travel but knows,
does not see but is clear,
does not strive but succeeds.

47

There is no reason to travel
to understand the world; no

reason to look out the window
to see the will of the sky.

The farther we go, the less
we know of ourselves.

Those free of themselves
learn without travel;
envision without looking;

accomplish without
going out of their way.

Without opening the door and leaving home,
you may come to begin to know the entire world.

Without gazing out the window,
you may see the transcendent revealing itself

in the commonplace, as the numinous in
the quotidian, as the luminous in the day-to-day,

as the plainness of dao.
If you were to leave, the farther you go, and with

each mile traveled, the less you will understand.
The sage reaches awareness

even before moving one step beyond the mat
before the doorway.

The practice of the sage is
to nourish vision, without looking, in order to see.

The sage labors, industriously, but
wisely, so that the work is done without the doing.

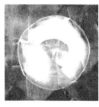

In study, there is daily benefit.
In dao, there is daily damage.

Lose and lose again,
all the way to nothing for nothing.
Nothing for nothing and nothing not for nothing.

Seeking the whole world, let nothing matter.
One who is busy cannot take on the whole world.

48

Study adds something day to day;
wisdom discards something day to day—

discarding, discarding,
until there is no reaching,
though all gets done.

The leader leads by never
attempting to lead.

Doing otherwise is embarrassing.

When one works with books, never a day
passes in which something is not learned.

When one engenders dao,
from the wilderness of one's inner stillness,

each day one lets go of one thing or another.
One experiences losing often and again—

until in achieving less, we find our true self.
Such is the path of non-action—

there is nothing
to attain, through the practice of quiescence.

When you do nothing, there is nothing that
remains to be done.

The best way to live in the world is
to allow the world to preside in its guidance—

whoever is not still will provide
a legion of obstructions, thrusting themselves

forward, in their impeding the way, as it moves
ceaselessly throughout the world.

The saint has no mind, because his mind is
the mind of the common people.

To the good, I am good.
To the not good, I am good too.

Virtue is good.

To the believer, I am a believer.
To the nonbeliever, I am a believer too

Virtue is belief.

The saint to the whole world is shy and humble,
to the whole world his mind is muddy.

The common folk turn
eyes and ears to him.

To everyone, he is a child.

49

The visionary's mind is said to be elsewhere—
however, it is dreaming the dream

of the common people.
I act with compassion towards those who are

decent and just.
Also, I act with compassion

towards those who are corrupt and fallen—
because grace is a blessing.

To those who exhibit faith, I am a believer in
their actions.

To those who are awash
in doubt, I also have faith that they may come

to believe—
since compassion is the blessing of active grace.

The visionary is
often provocative, but is also down-to-earth—

however, those in the world are confounded
by such a bewildering imagination.

Although, those same people are drawn
to the visionary without quite knowing why—

to all that listen to
the oracle of guidance that the starry-eyed one

offers, it sounds to them, as if it is the babbling
of a child.

Those free of themselves
have no preconceptions;
theirs is the mind of humanity.

To those kind to us,
we are kind;
to those unkind to us,
we are kind.

Therefore, all is kindness.

To those sincere with us,
we are sincere;
to those insincere,
we are sincere.

Therefore, all is sincerity.

Those free of themselves
appear indecisive, keeping
their minds open.

Everyone watches,
wondering.

Exit life, enter death.

Disciples of life are three in ten.
Disciples of death are three in ten.

Living people moving
into the territory of death
are also three in ten.

Why? Because they live.
Life is substantial.

Those who take life in and guard it well
can walk the path and not meet rhinos or tigers,
engage armies and not be wounded.

Rhinos have no place to sink their horns.
Tigers have no place to sink their claws.
Soldiers have no place to sink their swords.

Why? because they have no place for death.

5o

We take our departure through the door
into which we enter death—
devotees of life number three in ten;
as fellow partisans, we number

three in ten, in our march toward death;
ultimately, we are all protégés
of our elders—
passing through our lives, separately, or

in an enclave, into the illusory terrain of
life after death—
in this we also number three in ten.
Why can this be?

Because of living our lives with
the purpose of achieving a radiant body,
we have, instead, enlisted in pursuing
what is unwieldy, on the gross plane.

The one who cultivates an ability
to walk the path mindfully, avoids luring
rhinos and tigers by the smell of fear
that emanates to engage them.

The one who practices such mindfulness
will not be wounded in battle—
because rhinos can't find any place
to thrust their horns;

because tigers are
uncertain where they can rake their claws;
because soldiers don't see anywhere that
they can plunge their swords.

And why can this be?
Because those who live mindfully don't
leave any openings for which death
to transpire—since living in the present

is an aspect of our human inheritance—
our immortality.

We come out of the earth and live;
we die and enter the earth again.

Out of every ten,
three are out to
save their own lives,
three are out to kill.

Another three think they serve life,
but spread death instead. Why?
Because they are trying too hard.

But one in ten—that one walks
without danger, without
weapon or protection

because sharp edges
can do no harm.

Why? Because that one
does not serve death.

Dao creates, de nurtures.
Matter forms, power completes.

Among ten thousand things,
there is none that does not
honor dao and value de.
Honor dao value de.

Not fated, but in the nature of things,
dao creates, de nurtures.

Leading nurturing growing ripening tending sheltering.
Creating, not possessing. Doing, not presuming.

Leading, not ruling.
They say this is dark de.

5I

All things emerge from dao.
They are all engendered by de.

These are all formed into matter.
These are all patterned by nature.

So, the ten thousand things
mirror dao and echo de.

It is not required to mirror dao
and to echo de—

but they are inextricably woven
into the *helix* of all things.

So, dao arises prodigiously
in broad sweeps of primal force—

it is *the way;*
and de soars into tapers of smoke,

as sinuously as burning incense;
multiplies like blades of grass—

it is *active grace.*
Guiding, germinating, cultivating,

blossoming, evolving, preserving.
Producing but not owning.

Achieving attainment but not
expecting praise.

Indicating *the way*
without impeding natural *grace.*

This is elemental dark essence—
the intrinsic de of what is inherent.

The way of the creative universe
produces all things. In its effulgence,
it feeds all things. Each thing forms
according to its nature. Each thing
completes according to its condition.

In this way all things
honor the way,
joying in its fecundity.

Honoring the way,
celebrating its effulgence,
does not feel
like an obligation—

it is natural.

The way births, feeds, forms,
completes, maintains, increases.
The way does this, yet

claims no possession;
does no bragging or bossing;
looks for no control.

The way remains its own
mysterious production.

The beginning of the whole world
is the whole world's mother.

Grasp the mother to know the child.
Guard the mother, keep the body safe.

Stop talking, shut the door.
Life is full without a care.

Start talking, get busy.
Life is beyond hope.

See small, speak clear.
Guard gently, speak powerfully.

Use light. Turn and turn again to clarity.
Do not lose your body to calamity.

This is constant practice.

52

The way is mother of all.
When the mother is found,

we know the children,
knowing that good children
listen to their mother.

When we listen, we live
without exertion, without
even breathing hard.

Then, when breath stops,
there is nothing to fear.

The secret to clear-sightedness
is to see the small things;

the secret to strength is
embracing weakness.

Those who know the children
will know the mother and
see the light of the all.

The sluice
of the headwaters of the stream of the cosmos
mothers all that exists in this world.

If you acquaint yourself with the mother, you
may become familiar with her sons.
If you befriend her sons,

it is a sure way to remain
in contact with the touch of their mother—
in this find liberation from

the dread and certainty of death.
Keep your mouth closed, as if it were a locked
door.

Stand vigil, as a sentry,
over the vibrant perceptions of the senses.
Remain active in what you have devoted your

life to—
our lives open with even more breadth than
the sweep of our most far-reaching ambitions.

Finding the numinous in the commonplace
provides seeing what is large in what is small.
To acquiesce exhibits true power, as is

to yield is a sign of unassailable strength.
In making use of outer radiance, bring
this back within to turn this into discernment,

which turns again into intuition.
This will insure
your safety against being harmed, accidently.

The eminent definition of practice is—
the application of constant focus, the exercise
of indefatigable presence.

If I have enough sense,
my only concern will be
to walk on the main road.

The main road is easy, but
people love to be sidetracked.

The palace is spotless, but
the fields are full of weeds.

The granaries are empty.
They wear fine clothes,
carry sharp swords.

Sated with food and drink,
they have more than they need.
This is robbery, and it is not the way.

53

Were I asked to govern
according to the way,
first I would
work at humility.

The way is clear but
people choose alleys.

Look at the polished buildings.
Now notice that the fields
are rutted. This is why
your food is tainted.

Look at the elegant clothing;
at the impressive armaments;

see how the wealthy roll
in money and things—
name this

the extravagance of thieves.

This is the opposite of the way
of the creative universe.

If I could just exercise prudence enough,
the only care I might have

is to make sure to walk on the main road,
without the trepidation

of inadvertently drifting off and losing
my way.

Keeping to the main road
is said to be simple—however, people are

entertained by diversion, and often relish
distraction.

When the palace is impeccably kept, too
often, the fields are overgrown with

briars and nettles;
the silos of the granaries are left hollow.

Most people wear fashionable clothes;
others carry sheathed swords, visibly, on

their belts; many revel in gourmandizing
well past surfeit.

They all have
accrued possessions beyond imagination.

These are the members of the clique of
the plutocracy, tipsy on their own power.

This for sure, and absolutely for certain,
is not the way to follow dao.

What is well planted is not uprooted.
What is held well does not slip away.
It will be honored for generations.

Cultivated in the self, virtue will be real.
Cultivated in the family, virtue will overflow.
Cultivated in the village, virtue will grow.
Cultivated in the nation, virtue will be plentiful.
Cultivated in the whole world, virtue will be universal.

So observe self as self, family as family,
village as village, nation as nation, world as world.

How do I know the world is like this? Because of this.

54

What is planted with care does not uproot.
What is comprehended does not diminish.

That will be commemorated from one
generation to the next.

Nourish dignity within oneself and dignity
will be realized.

Nurture it in the family and dignity will be
as bountiful as a cornucopia.

Inculcate dignity within the lives of those
in the village and it will infuse the culture.

Foster dignity throughout the populace of any
nation and it will flourish among the masses.

Engender its grace across the boundaries
of the countries of the world

and it will reign, universally.
So, view your own body as itself.

See the family therein as the clan that it is.
Perceive the economy of the village

as being self-sufficient.
Recognize the nation as the working

coefficient for each and every individual
citizen.

Apprehend the multidimensional nature
of the universe as only a reflection

of the cosmos of your own mind.
So, how do I know

creation is augured in a way such as this—
by looking *and* seeing.

What is planted according to the way
cannot be uprooted;

what is grasped according to the way
cannot be snatched away or dropped.

With the way, the human chain
grows long and excellent.

Cultivation of excellence
in the self
creates integrity;

cultivation of excellence
in the family
creates abundance;

cultivation of excellence
in the community
creates compassion;

cultivation of excellence
in the nation
creates resilience;

cultivation of excellence
in the world
creates human flourishing.

Cultivation in the way
creates excellence in self,
family, community,
nation, and world.

How do I know this?
Look around you!

One who is full of virtue is
like a newborn child.

Insects don't sting.
Wild beasts don't pounce.
Birds of prey don't swoop.

Weak bones, soft muscles,
but his grip is firm.

He has not yet known
the union of male and female.

But he is whole,
and his spirit is full.

He cries all day but
does not grow hoarse.
This is perfect harmony.

Knowing peace is called endurance.
Knowing endurance is called enlightenment.

A life of profit is called lucky.
To breathe with your will is called strong.

The strong grows old.
This is not what is called dao.
What is not dao is finished early.

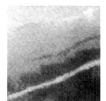

One who is replete with dignity is as radiant as an infant.
This is one whom hornets won't sting—

snakes will refrain from leaving their fang marks in anyone
such as this who strolls in bare feet through summer grass.

Wolves and coyotes will turn their
heads away when anyone such as this goes woodswalking.

A hawk, flying close over this one's head, merges with
this one's shadow, but does no harm.

Although muscles may hang limp from the thinness
of someone's bones, this one still offers a firm handshake.

This one has yet to experience the consummation of bliss
in the act of love; however, is complete, as is, in body.

This one is capable of sounding a shout across a gorge,
or over the rooftops, all day, without being discordant.

Such is the harmony of being in accord with dissonance.
Knowing consonance is

to stand with both feet in the steady stream of the brook.
Becoming one with the brook's constant

rush can be a breakthrough into the awakening of insight.
To profit in business

often requires racing about in order to be prosperous.
To need to breathe with exertion only leads to

one's exhaustion.
This is not any way to practice dao—trust that whomever,

or whatever, you are
in conflict with is a relationship that will not be enduring.

Followers of the way
are like babies—insects

do not sting them;
wild animals do not attack them;
birds of prey do not strike.

Like an infant, those
who follow the way
have flexible bones
and supple muscles.

They have a strong grip.

Innocent of distinctions
such as female and male,
they live naturally.

They can scream all day
without getting hoarse.
They are harmony itself.

For those following the way,
all is always harmony,
and wisdom is constant.

Flourishing is the outcome.

Knowledge of each breath
is the method.

Things grow, then decay;
this is the way of the way.

Whatever is contrary to
The way dies young.

Those that know don't tell.
Those that tell don't know.

Stop talking, shut the door.
Dull the edge, untangle the confusion.
Soften the glare, gather the dust.
This is called mysterious union.

It is not possible to embrace it.
It is not possible to neglect it.
It is not possible to profit from it.
It is not possible to harm it.
It is not possible to lift it up.
It is not possible to put it down.
So the whole world honors it.

56

Those who know
do not speak;
those who speak
do not know.

Those who know
close their mouths
and save their breath.

Those who know temper
the sharpness,
unraveling knots,
listening, harmonizing,

and creating agreement.
This is the mystery
of agreement.

Those who know
care nothing
for profit or loss;
riches or poverty.

These are those
free of themselves.

Those who possess a deep awareness don't paint
placards announcing it.

Those that need to announce it, really don't know.
Do your best by not speaking too often—

prudence is observed
most by not opening the space between your lips.

Protect yourself by not keeping the door to your
senses left ajar—

those instruments that clamor and swing—
they have a propensity,

to, put it simply, stir up trouble.
In anger, and especially, at ease, keep the edge

of your tongue blunt, rather than keeping it honed.
Soften the radiance of the aura of your delight—

it may be something that many do not understand.
Be at one with the dust—know the cleansing

qualities of humility.
This is known as the mystery of the flickering dance

of the union of twin flames.
Anyone who has experienced such rapture, has no

interest in charming enemies or aggravating friends,
either positive or negative; with dignity or disgrace—

this, as everyone in the whole world honors it,
is the absolute epitome of what it is to be human.

Rule straight, fight crooked.
Master the world with inaction.

How do I know this is so? Because of this.

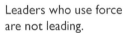

The more taboos,
the poorer the people.

The sharper the weapons,
the more confused the nation.

The craftier the people,
the stranger things become

The more rules,
the more crooks.

So the sage says, I take no action,
and the people change. I am quiet, and
the people are naturally upright. I do nothing,
and the people naturally become rich. I desire nothing,
and the people are naturally simple.

Leaders who use force
are not leading.

Leading requires doing nothing—
no pushing, no direction.

How do I know? Look around you—
pushiness creates poverty;
weapons create fear;
craftiness creates shady behavior…

The more attempts at control,
the less control exists.

This is why those free
of themselves say—

I will not coerce, and people
will transform themselves;

I will not intrude, and
people will prosper;

I will control my desires,
and everyone will do the same.

Govern a nation by adhering
to the ruled lines of equitable justice.
If there is the need to wage war,
stun your enemy by utilizing

unexpected means.
Gain mastery of the entire world
by USING THE FORCE—of inaction.
So, why do I know this as veritable

truth?
Because the more prohibitions
the more wretched the people;
the more powerful the weaponry

the further addled the nation;
the more scheming the people
the more peculiar the consequences;
the more legislators pass laws

that favor cupidity and greed
the more the plutocrats prosper.
So, what the sage recommends is:
I practice non-action and the people

eventually amend their ways;
I nurture quietude in my surroundings
and the people observe more ethical
customs;

I resolutely do nothing
and the people invest their time
in what is lucrative.
I do not entertain any desires,

whatsoever; and the people, well,
the people go about living their lives,
and find in what is unadorned
the inviolate mystery of nature.

58

Its politics silent, its people pure.
Its politics intrusive, its people abandon their posts.

Good fortune leans on disaster.
Disaster lurks beneath good fortune.

Who knows where they end?

Nothing is right.
Right becomes strange.
Good becomes monstrous.
People have been confused for a long time.
So the sage is an edge that doesn't cut,

pointed but not piercing,
straight but not excessive,
bright but not blinding.

When the bark of loudmouth politicians,
representing big business, ceases,

significant legislation can be passed,
as clear as an unpolluted stream, to benefit

the people.
When the nation's government is

obfuscated by politicians who are pawns of
the oligarchs, the people need to be shrewd.

Ecstasy banks its weight against the pillars
of heartbreak.

The pillars of heartbreak are intended to
hold up the porticos that

lend grace to the balustrades of happiness.
Who knows how long

such well-constructed architecture will last
before its façade crumbles into rubble?

There is no veracity—guilelessness changes
into chicanery.

Common decency becomes twisted, then is
transformed into sorcery.

People walk about as if they were
under the potent spell of a necromancer.

So, the sage is a blade that
doesn't sever—sharp but not penetrating;

unswerving but not
unconstrained; illumined but not dazzling.

Leaders who know themselves
lead people who practice wisdom.
A heavy hand creates pushback.

Sadness and happiness
sit side-by-side.
Happiness waits
inside sadness.

Who can know which
will happen when?

If force leads to fracture
and good implies bad,
does that mean there
can be no direction?

(It's easy to see why
people get confused!)

So it is that those
free of themselves
carve with the grain,
not against it—

cutting straight
without chopping.

The perfect square
has no corners.

59

Governing others, serving heaven,
there is nothing like restraint.

Restraint means planning ahead.
Planning ahead means storing up virtue.
Storing up virtue means nothing is impossible.

If nothing is impossible, no one knows the limit.
If no one knows the limit, a nation is possible.

The nation's mother may endure.
This means deep roots and a solid foundation,
Dao of long life and lasting vision

To be able to guide others and to esteem paradise,
nothing comes closer than acting with discrimination.

Discrimination personifies relinquishing oneself
to the efficiency of an organized system.

Relinquishing to an organized system promotes
the natural acquisition of a degree of dignity.

Acquiring dignity results in an awareness that there is
nothing that can't be achieved.

If there is nothing that can't be achieved,
then this posits that there is no point beyond which

one can go.
If there are no restrictions, then a person is capable

of governing a nation.
If a nation is governed judiciously, the power

of the feminine is elicited, which facilitates and insures
enduring prosperity.

This is known as the tradition
of putting down roots and establishing a burgeoning

of culture—such is
practicing the dao of longevity and provident foresight.

Gentleness best serves both
the self and others.

Only by gentleness do we see
the wisdom of harmony

in cultivating the self and
overcoming obstacles—

all obstacles that come by—
until we don't know

our own strength.

This is how to be a leader
and how to live a healthy life—

like a plant with deep roots
and a firm stalk.

60

Governing a great nation
is like a tasty little stir fry.

Attend to the world by means of dao,
and evil will have no power.

Not only is evil not powerful,
but its power will not harm people.

Not only will its power not harm people,
neither will the sage harm people.

The two will not harm one another.
Both are refreshed by virtue.

Leading a large group is like
cooking a small fish.

Lead according to the way
of the creative universe
and the demons are powerless—

not that they disappear,
but they can do no harm.

Since those free of themselves
do not hurt people,

no one gets hurt

when leaders lead
according to the way.

Guiding a nation to prominence
is similar to preparing a mouthwatering stir fry

of fresh garden vegetables.
Being present in the world through the practice

of dao always offers the best results.
In so doing, what is evil in the world loses its

dominance—
not that evil ever holds any dominion.

Not only will evil not hold any dominion,
but it will also not be able to

inflict any of its litanies of torments on anyone.
However, the sage, too, will be kept safe.

Neither the sage or the evil in the world will be
an affliction to one another, or the people in it.

The integrity found in
the practice of dignity is exhilarating to everyone.

A great nation is a watershed
at the confluence of the universe,
a deep gorge at the bottom of the world.

The female overcomes the male
by not moving lying low, still.

If a great nation gives way to a small state,
it will conquer the small state.

If a small state submits to a great nation,
it will be governed by the great.
So yield to take or yield and be taken.

A great nation only needs more people.
A small state only needs to join and follow others.

For both sides to get what they want.
the great nation should submit.

61

A country of prominence is as self-contained as
a watershed—with ranges
of mountains dividing its lakes and streams—
it is the amicable convergence of the cosmos;

it is the canyon at the center of the world
from which issues
the roar of the healing sound of rushing water.
All of this is under the influence

of the perpetual mystery of the Great Mother—
the female subdues the male
by becoming immobile; by sinking beneath him;
by practicing stillness.

If a country of prominence submits to
an emerging nation, it will vanquish the emerging
nation. If an emerging
nation submits to a nation of prominence, it will

vanquish the nation of prominence.
So, for those who seek to subdue another, they
do so by how much they relinquish and yield; and
those who seek to vanquish another also do so

through realizing just how to yield and relinquish.
All a country of prominence needs
is to be sure to care for its populace; consequently,
an emerging nation needs to emulate, and mirror,

the prosperity of its more prodigious neighbor—
each one is served by the other.
It is always to its own benefit, and others,
for a country of prominence to relinquish and yield.

A great nation
is like a low spot:

all streams run to it.

Consider that the low
is superior to the high

even though the low
might appear weaker.

Thus it is that a great nation,
listening to small nations,

gains friends, and the great
nation becomes greater.

The small nation considers
only its self/interest.

The great nation cares only
to unite and feed people—

greatness lies in lowliness.

62

Dao hides ten thousand things.
Good people treasure it.
For bad people, it is a sanctuary.

Pretty words might buy honor.
Pleasant actions might attract people.
Should bad people be abandoned?

When the emperor is enthroned
or public officials inaugurated,
though surrounded by discs of jade
and accompanied by teams of horses,
do not travel and enter this way.

Which of the ancients honored this way?
Don't you seek what you need
and escape when you are guilty?
Thus is the whole world honored.

Dao is concealed within the ten thousand things.
Those of virtue cherish it, and those who are

disenfranchised find asylum and solace in it.
Honeyed words might gain admiration.

Charming behavior may court people.
However, should you pass judgment on those

who are homeless that panhandle on the street?
So, when the emperor begins his reign,

during the coronation,
or government executives are being sworn in

at the dais, do not make superfluous gifts
of pendants of jade or a team of quarter horses.

However, from your own inner stillness,
make an offering of dao.

Why is dao so attractive to the initiate?
Is it because in it one discovers what one has

been casting about for years; and you are
absolved if you lose it, when you completely

forget about what you have
found? So, this is why everyone in the world

is exalted by it—
and the inner music of its own sweet rhapsody.

Of all the things that are,
the way is the most
respected of things
to the virtuous,

more valuable
than wealth.

The way does good
even to the bad.

Following the way
brings respect; even those
who do not follow it
gain from it.

So, when you see
the trappings of respect,
don't look for your own reward—

following the way is itself
all the respect you need.

Why did people
in the old days
respect the way?

Because it can be got
merely by the seeking—

nothing else required.

Even the guilty
are forgiven.

That is why it is
the most valuable
thing anywhere.

63

Do not do,
serve not serve,
taste not taste,

Great small many few,
reply to blame with virtue.

In what is hard, see what is easy.
In what is large, small.

The world's most difficult task
must start out easy.

The world's most important events
must start small.

The sage doesn't do anything to be big,
so he can achieve big things.

Easy promises require little faith.
Very easy must be very hard.

The sage does everything as if it were difficult
and thus finishes with nothing hard.

Enhance stillness—perform by not achieving.
Whet the palate with what cannot be tasted.

Observe what is significant in what appears
to be insubstantial.

Recompense condemnation with the dignity
of grace.

Find the transcendent in the commonplace.
Delight in the divinity of the everyday.

What the cosmos makes apparent is
that the enigmatic is accomplished with facility.

What is exponential and extraordinary
is comprised of what is an incremental harmony

of the cosmos.
The sage does not practice the art of non-action

for the ulterior motive of impressing others.
So, the attainment of the sage is substantial.

Facile vows make for mistrust.
Approaching life with indifference produces

one dilemma after another.
Since the sage meets the challenge of all

that turns out to be insurmountable difficulty
he never finds anything very hard.

To act without action
is the way of the way—

to do without worry;
to savor without gorging;

to see the big as small,
and the few as many;

to repay injury with kindness.

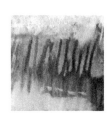

Those free of themselves see
difficulties when all is going well

and see little problems while
they are still little.

The huge arises from the tiny;
therefore, those free of themselves
do big things by doing small ones,

always with little effort.

Those who say "yes" quickly
seldom do what they say;

those who see everything as easy
find themselves in big trouble.

Those free of themselves
see the small things
and have no big worries.

What is tranquil is easy to hold.
What has not taken place
is easy to plan for.

What is brittle is easy to break.
What is tiny is easy to scatter.

Deal with it before it happens.
Put it in order before it is disordered.

A tree big as an embrace grows
from a shoot small as the tip of a hair.

A terrace nine stories tall
rises from a pile of dirt.

A journey of a thousand miles
begins when you put your foot down.

To act is to kowtow.
To grasp is to lose.

So the sage doesn't act and is not defeated,
doesn't grasp and is not mastered.

People fail when they've just begun to succeed.
So be as cautious at the end
as at the beginning,
and there will be no failure.

The sage therefore desires not to desire,
does not prize hard to get goods,
learns not to learn,

brings people back to what they passed by,
helps all beings do what is natural,
and does not dare to act.

64

A still thing is
easy to catch;

what has not arrived
is easy to stop.

The fragmented
is easy to scatter.

So, act before an event
has happened.

Order is best established
before disorder has begun.

The tree too large
to wrap your arms around
began as a tiny sprout;

the tallest tower rises
on a heap of dirt.

The journey of
a thousand miles

begins with a single
step.

Those acting for
their own benefit
do harm;

those who grasp
lose their hold.

Those free of themselves
do otherwise,
never rushing.

As much care of the end
as of the beginning
means success.
Those free of themselves
do not wish for what
others wish for, nor do
they overreach.

They desire what
others do not.

They see what
others miss.

They assist
the natural way of things,

never acting
for self alone.

What is still is simple to hold.
What can become a problem can be mastered
before it even begins to go awry.

The brittle shatters. The small is dispersed.
Learn how to handle the pot before its contents
boil and spill over.

Organize your papers to prevent confusion.
A tree, bearing the girth of a person's reach, rose
to its size from the wisp of a single seed.

The terrace, nine stories tall, was developed,
level by level, from a spade full of earth.
Placing just one foot forward can begin

a journey of a thousand miles.
The one who acts rashly insures his own defeat.
Anyone who exercises the need to hold on

secures losing whatever it was someone intended
to keep. So, the sage doesn't even make any
pretense of reacting—and suffers no loses at all.

Since one does not grasp at anything, there is
nothing to lose.
Know that people often need to deal with

the archetype of the saboteur on the very cusp
of achieving success.
Practice being as scrupulous at the end

as at the beginning—learn how to finish well.
This is the best insurance against failure.
So, the sage has no desire for any desires.

The sage doesn't bother
to acquire prized possessions.
The sage leads us back to what we think we have

lost; and offers relief to every being to do
what is natural and inherent within themselves—
but acts by not acting.

65

Ancient masters of dao
did not seek to enlighten people
but to keep them dull.

People are hard to control
if they are clever.

Those who use cleverness to govern
kill the nation.

Those who do not govern cleverly
are a blessing to the nation.

Those who know these two
also investigate style.

Investigating common style
is called dark virtue.

Dark virtue goes deep and far,
turns things inside out,
arrives at the highest obedience.

These ancient masters,
oh, they didn't reveal the path of dao to

illuminate the people.
The ancient masters, they kept quiet

about the light that shines along *the way*.
Why is it such a knotty

ordeal to provide appropriate guidance?
Is that because people often listen to it

but not always hear it?
If people rule with cunning and artifice,

they defraud and annihilate the nation.
Those who do not rule with

cunning and artifice, these people prove
to be a boon to the country.

These comprise the two polar opposites.
Those who know these two also delve

into what is fundamental and probe into
its method.

Fundamental method
is known as elemental dark essence—

and this
elemental dark essence, this is what

radiates in
perpetuity toward the harmonic whole.

Once upon a time
those who practiced
the way led centered,
grounded people.

Crafty leaders lead
crafty people,
and craftiness
is trouble.

Grounded leaders
are a blessing.
Remember this.

The way to find
right behavior is
deep contemplation.

This creates
the sort of leader
people want to follow.

The ocean can rule a hundred rivers
because it is good at lying low,
so it is king of a hundred rivers.

If the sage would be above the people,
he must speak as though he were below.

If he would be before the people,
he must put himself after them.

Thus the sage set over the people
is not heavy, is no disaster
set before them.

The whole world
happily pushes him forward
and does not despise him.

Because he does not compete.
there is no one in the world
who competes with him.

66

Because they are low,
rivers and seas drink
from mountain streams.

When it comes to leading,
be like that—be humble:

behind is actually in front.

In this way no one feels
oppressed. In this way
leaders are praised, not

blamed. When leaders
don't push, no one

pushes back.

The sea holds dominion over a hundred
brooks and rivers

because it succeeds in lying beneath them.
If the sage were to serve

as a guide in such a way,
he must do so by speaking to the people

with deference and modesty.
If the sage were to lead

the people, he would do so best by
placing himself at the rear of their ranks,

and to follow them from behind.
This is how the sage would govern—

without discouraging the people.
By his assuring the entire world

that by his representing them, such as
this, they will be made confident

that he will not abuse or deceive them.
So, the people find sustenance

in the sage, and refrain from becoming
weary of their expressing

their ardor for him.
Since the sage does not accept

the challenge of entertaining any rivals,
and because he does not act

as a competitor, then there is no one,
anywhere, who will compete with him.

Everyone in the whole world says
my dao is great, like nothing else.
Its greatness makes it seem different.

If it were the same,
it would have been
tiny all along.

I have three treasures
I hold and protect.
First is compassion.
Second is thrift.
Third is not daring to be
ahead of the whole world.

Compassion makes me brave.
Thrift makes me generous.
Not daring to be
ahead of the whole world
makes me a most useful tool.

Abandoning compassion to be brave,
abandoning frugality to be generous,
giving up being last to be first,
is to die.

Compassion wins every fight,
it is a sure defense.

Heaven help us
use compassion to protect.

67

Everybody around tells me that my dao
is so fine it is outstanding.
Because it is incomparable, that is what
makes it unique.

If it weren't so,
it would have dissipated some time ago.
I esteem three attributes above
all others that I cherish and venerate.

The first is active tenderness,
the second is providence, and the third
is not having the audacity to desire to
be ahead of everyone else.

Active tenderness makes me courageous;
economy makes me magnanimous; and
from modesty comes the wisdom to hold
dominion by being able to access guidance.

These days, most people eschew active
tenderness; they forgo providence;
however much they do attempt to exercise
thrift, they do not abide by modesty

because everyone wants to be first.
Accepting a dare such as this is suicide.
Active tenderness insures spiritual
strength; and offers the most resilience

to persevere.
This is the method through which
the divine watches over and nourishes
all of us.

Everyone knows the way
of the creative universe
is true, yet everyone calls
its teachings impossible.

Its impossibility is its truth.

I have three treasures—
humbleness, moderation, love.

With humbleness I can live
without expectations.
With moderation I can be generous.
With love I can be brave.

Too often we forget humbleness
and act only honorably.

Too often we forget moderation
and give only generously.

Too often we forget love
and act only bravely.

The outcome is death.

Love will be victorious,
even in battle; even in battle
love is the best protection.

The good warrior is not warlike.
The good fighter is not angry.
The good victor is not hostile.
The good commander is humble.

This is known as the virtue of not struggling.
This is known as using people's strength.
This is known as uniting with ancient heaven.

68

Wise leaders act
without aggression—
no anger, no attacking.

Wise leaders act
without assumption,

bringing out the
best in others.

Action without aggression
is in harmony
with all that is.

Therefore, it convinces others.
It is the ancient path of unity.

The most effective soldier is not savage.
The most powerful fighter is not enraged.
An honorable champion is not vindictive.

An inspiring leader
is known for possessing humility.
This is called practicing the art of dignity,

and then in honoring it by not making
such a great endeavor to achieve
its results.

This is the quality of being able to make
use of your own strength and to respect
the same in others.

Since ancient times, this has come to be
known as being in accord
with the highest purposes of divinity.

Among soldiers there is a saying:
I dare not master but play the guest.
I dare not advance an inch but withdraw a foot.
This is called not walking walking.

No arms holding,
no match throwing,
no army assembling.

There is no greater disaster than an easy rival.
With an easy rival, I lose what I treasure.
Thus when soldiers join battle,
the one who mourns wins.

It's wiser to be
a guest than a host.

It's wiser to retreat a foot
than advance an inch—

this is advancing
without aggression;

this is vigilance
without weapons;

this is victory
without fighting.

No disaster is greater
than thoughtless violence.

Doing just the opposite
wins every time.

69

Among soldiers there are the adages—
RESIST MAKING THE FIRST MOVE, PREFER TO BE

THE GUEST; and
DO NOT ADVANCE AN INCH, WITHOUT WITHDRAWING

A SINGLE FOOT.
This has come to be known as marching

in place; or
not showing your arms after rolling up

your sleeves; and not launching
an attack, but still capturing the enemy.

There is no tragedy more poignant than
the miscalculation of minimizing

one's opponent.
By trivializing and underplaying

one's adversary, the soldier nearly forfeits
any, or all, advantage.

So, when the troops become joined in
combat, and the smoke of battle ensues,

the one who bleeds both blood and sorrow,
and whose wails of mourning can be heard,

standing among the fallen,
THAT IS THE ONE who will be said to have won.

My words are easy to know,
easy to do. But there is no
one in the whole world
that knows, none who do.

Words have an ancestor.
Action is master.

Because people do not know,
they do not know me. The one who
knows me is rare, so I am highly valued.

The sage wears rough cloth
and keeps jade in his heart

70

My words are easy
to understand, easy
to practice, yet so
few practice them.

My words originate
in the origin—
the motions of
the universe itself—

yet so few follow
my words, so few
follow the way.

Those who know
are rare, a treasure.

Outside, they wear
rags, but inside—there
is precious jade.

These words of mine—
they are simple to understand, distinct,

and straightforward, easy to carry out
and act upon.

However, I am not aware of one person
who possesses a clear sense of them,

or who realizes what they actually mean.
These words—

their origin and source are of an ancient
tradition.

They inflect upon my actions—
they inform all that I do and don't do.

It is because people are not able to
discern fully, that they look past me

even when they believe they think they
know who I am.

So, the ones who comprehend are few,
if not rare, in number.

As I am honored in such a manner, I am
also treated with equal amounts of

misapprehension by those who choose to
be brutes and strong-arm misconceptions.

This is why the sage is often seen wearing
threadbare clothes, but keeps a jade

medallion that reflects the light of THE WAY
polished and gleaming within his heart.

Know
not know
highest.

Not know
know
sickness.

The sage is not sick
because he is sick of sickness.

Sick of sickness,
he is not sick.

7I

Knowing that we do not know—
that is the greatest achievement.

Not knowing when
we think we know
is a sickness.

Being sick of this sickness
is the only way to health.

Those free of themselves heal
because they see the disease.

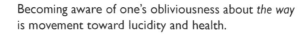

Becoming aware of one's obliviousness about *the way*
is movement toward lucidity and health.

Becoming indifferent about acquiring such knowledge,
in one's best interest, is practicing a kind of idiocy that

invites one malady after another.
If one is indisposed to just one more malady, then

the illness of ignorance is in process of being cured.
The sage is not ill because he is not predisposed to

such maladies—the sage is not only healthy, but he is
also not ailing from the affliction of ignorance of *the way*.

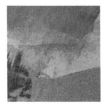

72

When people do not fear power,
vast regulation arises.

Do not disrespect their homes.
Do not loathe the places they live.

If they are not objected to,
they will not object.

The sage is self aware
but does not appear so,

loves himself
but is not self indulgent.

He lets that go when he takes this.

When people lose their ability to experience *the ahness*
of wonder, or to give consideration to what they fear,

grave misfortune occurs—often followed by what are
severe restrictions and prohibitions.

Do not be contemptuous of where some people call
home.

Do not allow anyone to be so disdained that they are
bullied in the workplace.

If people are not provoked, then
they will not reciprocate with any further provocation.

So, the sage is conscious, but does not display, or make
trick exhibitions, of consciousness.

Oh, the sage, what the sage exercises is approbation by
esteeming the *self* within the *self,* without egotism and

pride—what the sage
augurs is relinquishing that when wisely selecting *this.*

When we fear
the wrong things,
bad things happen.

Do not constrict your heart;
do not ignore your calling,
lest you become tired of life.

Those free of themselves
know themselves but say
nothing of it;

they take care of themselves,
yet do not value the self.

In this way, they gain
this
without losing

that.

To be brave and daring means killing.
To be brave and not daring means living.
These two may be good may be bad

What heaven despises, who knows why?
It is difficult even for the sage

Dao of heaven
does not struggle but is victorious,
does not speak but is charitable,
is not summoned but comes,
revises but has a plan.

Heaven's web is all-encompassing,
sparse but nothing is lost.
Sometimes one who is fearless and bold
will either be killed or need to kill to survive.

73

Sometimes one who is intrepid and daring
will be certain to choose to save lives.

Between these two, which one
is the superior choice, which the deleterious?

Divinity is intolerant of various things.
Who can say why?

Even for the sage, this is not easy to discern.
Divine dao does not endeavor,

but it is triumphant.
It does not utter a word, but is benevolent.

It does not call or question, but comes forth
and replies.

It does not petition,
but is provided with whatever it requires.

Unconcerned, it apparently is tended to by
unseen hands.

The mesh of the net of the divine opens
over vast spaces;

although it may look rough-hewn, nothing
evades the matrix of its woven cords.

Fearlessness gets you killed;
care keeps you alive;
one is good; one is bad.

Who knows why
the cosmos does
as it does?
Those free of themselves
keep their eyes open.

The way of the creative universe
does not push, yet it pushes through.

It does not speak, yet
it is always heard.

It does not call,
yet all come to it...

eventually.

The way of the creative universe
is relaxed, yet its designs

work and work.

The sky's net is far-flung
and the holes in it are huge,

yet nothing
ever
escapes.

People are not afraid to die,
so why threaten them with death?

If some people fear death
but still act perversely
and we kill them,
who will dare?

There is an official executioner.
Acting like an executioner is
like trying to take the place of the carpenter.
Play at being a carpenter, and you are
sure to injure your hand.

74

If people do not fear dying, it is
of no use to intimidate anyone by threatening

to kill them.
If people possess a terminal fear of death, but

intentionally commit an unlawful and depraved
act, that insures them that they will face

execution, who, then, ventures to risk being so
defiant?

Perennially, there is always someone who
will assume the role of putting people to death.

If you should be of such an audacious
character to even remotely fantasize of taking

on the role
of executioner, it will be similar to that of your

impersonating a skilled carpenter, in operating
a wood saw.

If you presume to try to saw the wood, as does
the carpenter, with craft

and precision—you just may gouge your hand,
or even, mistakenly, lose a finger.

What is the point
of threatening death
to those who do not fear it?

When justice is just
who does wrong?

Always, there is
a judge and
an executioner.

Like a carpenter's apprentice,
the unpracticed executioner
will have bloody hands.

The people are hungry.
Because those on top tax them heavily,
thus they are hungry.

People are unruly.
Because those on top interfere,
thus they are unruly.

People take dying lightly.
Because those on top demand so much,
thus people think little of death.

Having nothing to live on,
there is no point in honoring life.

75

Why do the people starve?
Because those who govern consume the proceeds from taxes.

So, the people go hungry.
Why are the people contentious, and why do they lift up their

truculent cries?
Because those who often rule impede common human rights

and hamper economic mobility.
So, the people roam the streets in disorderly throngs, venting

their obstreperous epithets.
Why do the people place so little weight on dying?

Because
those in control press for too much and insist on subservience.

So, the people see life as specious and consider death as an exit
from a life of misery—having so little to live for,

and exist on, there are few reasons
to be found to extol anything, or any need to glorify life, at all.

Why do people starve?
Because hierarchy
takes their food.

That is why they starve.

Why do people rebel?
Because the powerful oppress.

That is why they rebel.

When do people live well?
When they have something to live for.

That is when they live well.

Life goes well when
all goes lightly.

76

A person born soft and supple
dies hard and stiff.

Vegetation born soft and crisp
dies dried up and rotten.

The strong and hard are disciples of death,
the soft and supple disciples of life.

The soldier that struggles is defeated.
The tree that struggles snaps.

The big and strong fall.
The soft and supple rise.

A person is born pliant and limber.
At our death we are rigid and cold as a stone.

The leaves of plants and trees emerge pliant
and fresh in color.

However, at the end of their cycles they are
desiccated and fetid.

So, what is unyielding and inflexible become
the dire adherents of death.

And the lithe and supple are the proponents
of life.

Every soldier, who lacks resilience, endeavors,
as though marching through thick mud,

but is defeated.
A tree, whose branches are withered

and brittle, are easily broken.
The resistant and stalwart will occasion to fall.

The flexible and yielding that spring up—it is
they who flourish.

When we are born,
we are soft and supple;
when we die,
we are rough and stiff.

Everything is like this—
plants are soft and supple,
then rough and stiff.

Life is soft and supple.
Death is rough and stiff.

The rough and stiff tree
will be getting the ax.

Those who rely on rough
and stiff do not last—

soft and supple
overcomes.

Dao of heaven –
how like stringing a bow.

What is high is pressed down,
what is low is raised up.

Where there is too much, it is diminished.
Where there is too little, it is supplemented.

Dao of heaven
diminishes surplus,
supplements what is lacking.

Human dao is different.
It takes from what is lacking
and adds to surplus.

Who has more than enough and
gives to the whole world?
Only one on the way.

The sage does not rely on doing,
accomplishes with no office,
does not desire to appear worthy.

77

Dao of heaven so much resembles stringing
a bow—

taut enough to offer
pluck, loose enough to bend, with resilience.

What is high is brought down,
what is modest is elevated, in prodigiousness

and esteem.
If the bow string is too long, it is altered; if

it is too short, it is augmented and increased.
Dao of heaven reduces surfeit,

adds to whatever is absent or gone missing.
Human dao differs so—

not incrementally, but exponentially.
In the human realm, the ones that already

possess, then chance to possess more,
extract and seize from those who subsist on

less and less, and who never know plenty.
Who is the one who has more than others,

and shares the excess with everyone
in the world?—only one who is practicing

the way.
So, the sage does not rely on accolades—

but is nurtured from within, by what is real
about the true work.

The sage attains achievement
without abiding on claims to its importance.

Oh, the sage develops
a skill to trade away such kudos for modesty.

The way of the universe
is like stringing a bow:

the top comes down,
the bottom goes up.

Just so the creative universe
takes from what has a lot,
gives to what has little.

It is the way
to give and to take.
People do not do this—

we take without giving.

Who among us takes,
then gives to all?

The one who
knows the way of
the creative universe!

Those free of themselves
act without preconception;

do what needs to be done
without calculation.

Those free of themselves
have no need to be
considered extraordinary

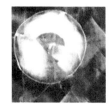

In the whole world there is nothing weaker than water,
but for attacking the strong and powerful
there is none that can surpass it.
Nothing can change it.

Weak overcomes strong,
soft overcomes hard.

The whole world probably knows this,
but no one practices it.

78

So the sage says *who accepts*
the nation's disgrace is called fit to rule. Who
takes on the nation's disasters is master of the universe.

Straight talk seems inside out.

In all the world, there is nothing more
submissive than water.

However, for assailing
what is hard and dominant nothing can

surpass or exceed it.
This is known as an immutable law.

What is weak subdues what is strong.
What is acquiescent and compliant

outlasts what is rigid and firm.
Everyone in the entire world probably

does not doubt this,
but who makes use of this in their lives?

So, the sage advises:
THE ONE WHO ASSUMES THE NATION'S

DISHONOR AND SHAME IS SUMMONED
TO GOVERN.

THE ONE WHO ACCEPTS THE BURDEN OF NATIONAL CATASTROPHE—
THAT ONE BECOMES A LUMINARY AND IS REGARDED AS A PRINCE.

What is heard to be true often exhibits
a different echo than what is expected;

what contradicts itself often enough is
not false;

and what are apparent opposites, well,
many times, they are truer than fiction.

When a big quarrel is resolved,
some complaint must remain.

What is the virtue of announcing resentment?
What is the virtue of believing error?

The sage keeps his part of the bargain
but lays no claim on other people.

The virtuous person honors the agreement.
Those without virtue exert control.

Dao of heaven is impartial
but stays with good people

79

When two opposing views attempt to reconcile,
what remains

is more than just a modicum of consternation.
Consequently, to what

purpose is there to proclaim pique or bitterness?
And what is the benefit of holding on

to the indignity from the effrontery of another?
It is the sage who honors

the sacred contract of not taking up resentment
and striking back at the other.

One who is rooted in
dignity and esteem retains perspective and stands

tall before others.
However, the one lacking control

and discernment, and who is overrided by viscera,
cannot recognize such a humane agreement.

Dao is active divinity,
neutral and detached, ever-present in everyone

at all times—it is just whether or not we develop
the capacity to invoke the grace to access it.

If a grudge remains
after a reconciliation
what is accomplished?

Those free of themselves
seek reconciliation without
pushing their opponents.

Those who follow the way
of the creative universe
do more than what is
favorable to themselves.

The way cares for no side
except that of the good.

Small nation, few people.

Let there be tools that are not used.
Let the people be serious about death and not travel far.

Though there are boats and carriages,
they have no use for them.

Though they have armor and troops,
they do not display them.
Let people return
to the knotting of ropes.

Their food pleasant.
their clothes pleasing.
their homes safe.
happy with their customs.
they live within sight of the neighboring country,
hear each others chickens and dogs.
People die in old age
with no to and fro.

A small nation is one of few people.
Although there is engineering that automates

the combines more efficiently than hand
tools, they are of no use.

These people respect the finite nature
of their lives, and they do not journey far.

There are well-made boats and carriages,
but no one rides in them.

There is armor fashioned, and a stockpile
of weapons,

but there are no marching orders.
The people replace the art of writing with

the craft of weaving ropes
that are displayed in the skillful twist and

loop of knots.
Their food is nourishing; their clothes are

practical; their homes are architecturally
sound.

They are content in the practice of their
ways; although they reside

in close proximity to the border of their
neighbors in an adjoining country.

The crowing of roosters and the woofing
of dogs resound

on their side of the border.
These people live without conflict

or discord—they
live until old age and die a peaceful death.

An ideal nation would be small,
with a small population.

It would be simple, with
no need of complications.

Yes, it would have boats
and carriages, yet the people
would be too busy living
to make use of them—

they would treasure their lives
so much they would be too busy
to think of going anywhere.

Those citizens would forget
writing and take up braiding.

They would consider
the simplest food best;

the plainest clothing
beautiful; the simplest
homes enough, and simple
enjoyments plenty.

For those people,
even if another nation
were in sight, so close

they could hear the songs
of birds and barks of dogs,

they would take no interest
in it, all their contented lives.

Trustworthy words are not pretty.
Pretty words are not trustworthy.

The good don't argue.
Those who argue are not good.

Those who know don't play games.
Those who play games don't know.

The sage does not accumulate.
The more he does for others, the
more there is.
The more he offers others, the
more there is.

Dao of heaven –
do good and do not harm.

Dao of the sage –
act without struggle.

81

Sincere words are not fancy;
fancy words are not sincere.

The good do not quarrel;
the quarrelsome do no good.

Learning will never grasp
the way of the creative universe—

grasping does not lead to wisdom.

Those free of themselves
do not hold back—the more
they give, the more they have.

They give all and so
possess everything.

The way gives,
never harming.

Those wise in the way
never take, but only add.

Reliable words that exact truth sometimes lack aesthetics.
Aesthetic words that express what is genuine

may not always be reliable.
Those who are wise, and whose actions originate

from their center, do not quarrel.
And those who are contentious are not only unwise but

they can also be as dishonorable as they are disagreeable.
The sage is never one to accrue

or collect anything—either bad or good, except maybe
rainwater.

The practice
of the sage, is to do as much that can be done for others—

which only increases the inner wealth of all.
The more the sage

gives to others, the more abundance there is to keep on
giving.

Dao of heaven
is incisive, but the diamond of its divinity never does any

harm.
Dao of the sage, always with the propensity of being active,

if only
it is accessed, through the PRACTICE OF NO PRACTICE, is—

not to endeavor; but to move in harmony with
what is without and within—the greater force of nature.

dao: oklahoma, april

a squall doesn't last all day

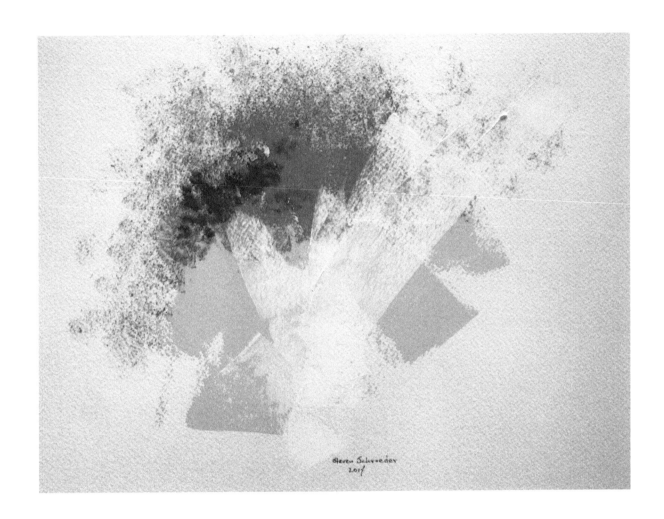

Steven Schroeder
2015

dust and light

between heaven and earth

from what I've tasted of desire

elements 1

elements 2

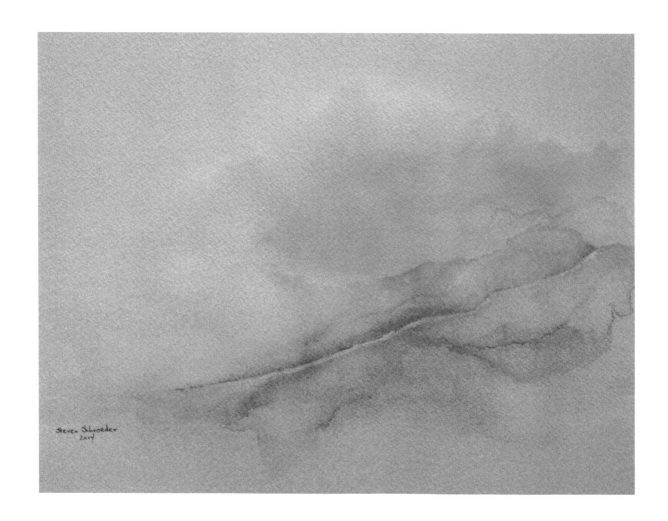

ninety miles of nothing

nothing makes it work

a door we call the world

CPSIA information can be obtained at www.ICGtesting.com
Printed in the USA
LVOW02s2116010415

432903LV00033BA/219/P

9 780991 532179